WHY THE MASS MATTERS

WHY THE MASS MATTERS

A Guide to Praying the Mass

Gerard Moore

BOOKS & MEDIA
Boston

Nihil Obstat: Rev. B. Byron, DD, MTh.

Imprimatur: ✠ David Cremin, DD, VG

May 7, 2004

Library of Congress Cataloging-in-Publication Data

Moore, Gerard, 1956-

   Why the Mass matters : a guide to praying the Mass / Gerard Moore.
— 1st North American ed.

       p. cm.

   Originally published: Strathfield, Australia : St. Pauls Publications, 2005.

   ISBN 0-8198-8309-3 (pbk.)

   1. Mass. I. Title.

   BX2230.3.M66 2006

   264'.02036—dc22

2005x019461

The Scripture quotations contained herein are from the *New Revised Standard Version Bible: Catholic Edition,* copyright © 1989, 1993, Division of Christian Education of the National Council of the Churches of Christ in the United States of America. Used by permission. All rights reserved.

Cover design by Rosana Usselmann

Cover photos—background: Brandxpictures\Inmagine; people: Corbis.

First published in 2004 by St. Paul's Publications, Strathfield, Australia.

First North American Edition, 2006

"P" and PAULINE are registered trademarks of the Daughters of St. Paul.

Published by Pauline Books & Media, 50 Saint Paul's Avenue, Boston, MA 02130-3491. www.pauline.org

Printed in U.S.A.

Pauline Books & Media is the publishing house of the Daughters of St. Paul, an international congregation of women religious serving the Church with the communications media.

1 2 3 4 5 6 7 8 9   12 11 10 09 08 07 06

Contents

Acknowledgments

MY THANKS TO THE Australian Catholic Social Justice Council for allowing me to rework material I wrote for them in the booklet *Eucharist and Justice*. As well, similar thanks to Margaret Press, editor of *Eucharist: Faith and Worship*, for allowing me to incorporate some of my contributions from that publication.

Excerpts from the English translation of the *General Instruction of the Roman Missal* copyright 2002 and the *General Introduction to the Lectionary* copyright 1981, International Commission on English in the Liturgy, Inc., all rights reserved, are used with permission.

Finally, it would be remiss of me not to mention those who have read this book closely in its various drafts. In particular, I would like to thank Pat Flannagan, Kris Sanotti, and Ursula O'Rourke. Their comments were all welcomed, but the responsibility for the final product rests with the author.

Introduction

HOW ARE WE TO APPROACH THE MASS—the summit of
the formal, public prayer (or *liturgy*) of the Church,
which is also referred to by the ancient name, the
Eucharist (from the Greek word for "thanksgiving")?
Try seeing the Mass as a garden: to know a garden, we
have to go into it. Once we do that, we find ourselves
among different plants, colors, scents, sounds, and
textures. Some of these form spectacular highlights,
others quiet moments of calm. There are features that
constantly attract us, along with others that occasionally surprise us. The more we move along the paths
and between the beds, the more ways we are touched.
That's how a garden matters. So how does the *Mass*
matter?

Like a garden with many plants and other features,
the Mass, or Eucharist, includes many prayers and
other parts or actions (rites). Each individual part has
its own dynamism and energy. Some require gesture
and movement, others speech or song, still others eating and drinking, while attitudes of silence and won-
der should never be far away. Sometimes there is rich

contrast between succeeding rites, at other times the celebration moves smoothly, almost imperceptibly, from one part to the next. Ancient documents provide a trusted witness to which features of the Mass should be highlighted, while history, local customs, cultural shifts, and our own piety reflect other concerns and provide ample and colorful backdrops and decorations.

The present book is something like a walk through a celebration of the Mass. We will try to get inside each of its respective parts, see what they ask of us, and relate them to the celebration of the Mass as a whole. While there may well be some surprises in store (which garden has no surprises?), our overarching aim is to learn how to pray the Mass better, that is, by praying it *fully*—by attending to all its parts, not neglecting any; *consciously*—by being present to all the sensations and meanings of what we, the entire assembly of the faithful, do; *actively*—by engaging our hearts, minds, and bodies throughout the celebration; and *lovingly*—by responding generously to what it calls us to remember to be and to do.

To begin though, perhaps it is better to cast our minds back to a time much earlier than our own. The basic structure of our current Mass is really quite ancient: we can see it in the writings of a famous second-century Christian author, Justin Martyr (c. 100–c. 165). A philosopher, he was converted to Christianity around the year 130. Twenty years later he was putting his intellectual skills to good use, writing a defense of this newly emerging religion for the emperor. Known as the *First Apology,* his defense contains our earliest surviving account of the Eucharist. In it he includes two descriptions of the Mass. By combining them, we create a window through which we can see how the first generations of believers worshiped. Of course, being as ancient as they are, predating the split in the Church in the eleventh century, such descriptions lie at the base of the Liturgy of the Eucharist in both the West (the Catholic Church) and in the East (the Orthodox Churches).

This is how Justin prayed the Mass:

On the day named after the sun, people who live in the cities and in the country gather for a common celebration. Then the writings that the apostles have left or the writings of the prophets are read, as long as time allows. After the reader finishes his task, the president gives an address in which he urgently admonishes the people to follow these excellent teachings in their lives. Then we all stand up together and offer prayers...bread, wine, and water are brought and the president offers up prayers and thanksgiving—as much as he is able. The people assent by speaking "Amen." Then the things over which thanks has been said are distributed to all who are present, and the deacons take some to those who are absent. In addition, those who are well-to-do give whatever they wish. Whatever is collected is kept by the president, who uses it to help widows and orphans.[1]

From this general glimpse of how the Mass was celebrated in Justin Martyr's time, we are able to explore its more specific, constituent parts. In doing this though, note that the Eucharist is an *action* (as opposed to a mere spectacle to be witnessed) of the *Christian assembly* (a gathering of the baptized or faithful) on a Sunday (the day of our Lord's resurrection). Hence, once the baptized have gathered on a Sunday, they celebrate with:

- scriptural readings;
- a homily based on the readings;
- the prayer of the faithful;
- the sign of peace;
- the presentation of the gifts;
- the prayer of thanksgiving;
- Communion to all present and to those unable to attend;
- and a collection for the poor.

Compared to our contemporary Order of Mass, this list contains a few surprises. Some of our favorite elements, such as a Penitential Rite or Creed, are not present, yet other parts, such as the prayers of the faithful and the sign of peace, which would seem to be recent innovations, can be seen to date from ancient times. Hence, over history and across cultures, the basic pattern handed onto us by Justin has been expanded and developed. However, at various times in the past, certain modifications have tended to obscure the focus of the celebration. But just what is that focus?

The Fountain at the Center of the Garden

Through our active participation in the Eucharist, we are led more deeply into *the presence of Christ.* His presence is made manifest to us in a variety of ways as the liturgy unfolds, in ways which build on each other. The Church document setting out the principles and norms for interpreting and celebrating the Mass, the *General Instruction of the Roman Missal* (GIRM or *General Instruction*) is most clear about these different modes of Christ's presence. Christ is present in the *assembly* that gathers in his name, but also in the person of the *ordained minister,* in the *Scriptures,* and in the *Eucharistic elements,* that is, the consecrated bread and wine (GIRM, no. 28). However, the high point of our participation in the entire celebration is near its conclusion: our *Communion* in the Body and Blood of Christ. But this is to take us to the end of the present book too quickly!

Our survey of the Mass, which will refer to its various contemporary forms, will be based on the current edition of the *Roman Missal* (the official text of the Mass liturgy), released in Latin in 2002. This document describes the Mass as having four parts: 1) the Introductory Rites (see Chapter 1); 2) the Liturgy of the Word (Chapter 2); 3) the Liturgy of the Eucharist (Chapters 3, 4 and 5); and 4) the Rites of Dismissal (Chapter 6).

As well as the Missal or text of the Mass, there is the *General Instruction of the Roman Missal*. It either precedes the *Roman Missal* in the one publication or is published as a separate document. Note that the numbering of the Instruction's paragraphs differs between editions, for example, the numbering in the 2002 version of the *General Instruction* differs from that in the previous (1975) edition. The references in this book are based on the *2002* version.

As well as encountering references to this *Instruction,* we will encounter two other relevant official texts, namely, the *General Introduction to the Lectionary* (GIL) and the *Directory for Masses with Children* (DMC).

Now, the Mass may take a variety of forms, depending on the options that a group who is planning a liturgy chooses from the Missal. Such a variety of options reflects the flexibility inherent in the Roman tradition. According to the *General Instruction* (no. 352), the options are provided for pastoral effectiveness and the common spiritual good of the people. But how do we actually choose the best options for any particular celebration of the Mass? Some options, so we are guided, should be chosen to enhance the correspondence between the readings, prayers, and songs, on the one hand, and the needs, spiritual preparation, and aptitudes of the assembly, on the other. Also, the presiding priest should pay attention to the spiritual good of the people, rather than merely favor his own personally preferred options. Liturgy planners (including ordained ministers) are also advised to choose among options in consultation with members of the assembly. This ideally should lead to a harmonious celebration by *all* those gathered. By thus exercising appropriate options in consultation with a variety of the assembly's members, we hope to foster *communion*. This is central to praying the Mass.

Throughout this book, we will encounter many of the options provided within the different parts of the Mass. At this point, it is also worth noting that the *Missal* provides us with many optional *settings* of the Mass, that is, particular *combinations of options* suited to specific occasions, such as: Masses for the laity, the election of a pope; for martyrs, holy women and men, refugees and exiles; and for justice, peace, times of famine and drought. Over a period of months, such settings contribute to a richness and vitality in our worship.

While our primary concern will be to learn how to pray the Mass better, we can see from our brief survey of some of Justin Martyr's work that it is helpful to be familiar with the history of the Mass. Accordingly, I have included a thumbnail sketch of the major periods in the development of the liturgy (see Chapter 9).

Also, as a further aid to our study, I have appended a glossary of selected terms. Finally, I have listed some resources for further exploration.

And so, let us proceed along the path through the rites that make up the Mass.... How does the Mass *matter*?

Chapter 1

The Introductory Rites

THE ENTRANCE RITES SEEK TO gather all the people who enter the assembly and form them into a community, a community that is the body of Christ. This is no simple task, and our liturgy provides many different ways to do this.

We tend to underestimate the importance of assembling even though it has a number of significant moments. In a sense, the Mass "begins" as we turn our minds to leaving home and traveling to the church, and it continues and is filled out as we enter the building together, giving substance to the body of Christ.

We open our celebration and strengthen our unity with the song that accompanies the procession of the priest and ministers. This procession brings the assembly a sense of wholeness; and through it the priest, deacon, and ministers take their places in the body. The *Book of the Gospels,* when it is carried in, is placed on the altar, highlighting the presence of Christ in his word. Then, as the entrance song comes to a conclusion, four small, but highly significant gestures take place: the veneration of the altar, the Sign of the Cross, the greeting, and the introduction.

The Veneration of the Altar

All the members of the entrance procession bow before the altar (GIRM, no. 122), which the priest and deacon then kiss. This is the first of three distinctive kisses in the liturgy.

Christian tradition has often understood the altar as a sign of Christ. When the ordained ministers kiss the altar they point forward to the actions and prayers that will be said at this table through which Christ will become present for our eating and drinking in Communion.

The Sign of the Cross

Once the procession has concluded, the first action of the entire assembly is the Sign of the Cross. At its heart, this is the physical act of marking our bodies with the marks of Jesus' death. Each of us makes the gesture, and all of us make it together.

But when we mark our bodies with this sign, are we really aware of what we are doing? Are we not suggesting that we will stand where Jesus stood—that where his cross is, there we will be? This may be a more challenging task than we imagine at first. It is worthwhile, then, revisiting Jesus' last days to discover what it means to be at his cross.

Jesus' passion (sufferings unto death) involved a violent, relentless stripping of his identity as a human being. Scourged, mocked, and naked, he walked in solidarity with those in society who were outcasts and the recipients of others' derision. In all this he was left friendless. He walked with the abandoned. Carrying his own cross, he became a public spectacle for his own people. His rejection was complete. His death was a public sport. His religious leaders betrayed him. His crucifixion was at the hands of the enemy, and it was associated with the crucifixion of criminals. His burial was rushed, with less than proper arrangements, without custom or dignity. Even in death Jesus was a nuisance, disrupting the temple worship. It fell to a nonbeliever to provide for him.

When we mark our bodies with the Sign of the Cross we symbolize the suffering of Christ. We also symbolize our commitment to those in the same position as him. In his passion, Jesus was stripped of human dignity. In the Sign of the Cross we make a commitment to stand in solidarity with those whose human dignity is under threat. In the passion, Jesus endured the wrath of the mob, the violence of society, and the desertion of his companions. In the Sign of the Cross we ask about the underside of our own society, the scapegoating, the violence, the cowardice. We declare that it should cease. In his death, Jesus is among criminals, helpless bystanders, and women rendered powerless by their society. In the Sign of the Cross we say that such people shall never be without help—our help.

Since the thirteenth century we have clothed the sign with the words of Baptism. Those words recall our own entry into the community of Christ's kingdom. They signify our joy in the resurrection, our belonging to the Church, and our commitment to embody the kingdom of God on earth. Through the Sign of the Cross the gathered assembly marks itself as dedicated by Baptism to stand by the cross of Jesus.

The Greeting

Complementing the Sign of the Cross are the presiding priest's words of greeting. He may choose them from a range of formulae. By leading an exchange with the assembly, he makes clear his role, as presider, of calling all present to prayer. The people's response to this call is essential. Not only does it give voice to their willingness to participate in the Eucharist, it is a reminder that the Mass is the action of the whole assembled body of Christ. The responses of the body then are essential to the celebration, not merely an added extra (GIRM, nos. 34, 35).

The Introduction to the Mass of the Day

At this point in the Introductory Rites, the *General Instruction* offers a most intriguing possibility: either the presiding priest, the deacon, or a lay minister may introduce the gathered faithful to the Mass of the day (GIRM, no. 50). Such an introduction should enable us to engage more fully in this particular liturgy, yet be brief, not drowning the community in superfluous words. At the same time, the introduction points out the variety of roles that different people in the gathered assembly will assume. This is quite important. From the first minutes of the Mass, the liturgy brings to our attention the variety of ministers and ministries. This should help us rethink our over-reliance on only the priest: we often characterize him as the only minister. Furthermore, the introduction allows the presiding priest the opportunity to step back, so that his role does not dominate.

The Penitential Rite

Such pastoral openness, choice, and variety in ministries evident in the introduction to the Mass of the day flows over into the Penitential Rite. However, there is a tendency to identify the rite too narrowly with personal sin and the need for individual forgiveness. In part, this stems from the origin of the rites. From the early Middle Ages the celebrant offered private prayers of unworthiness as he approached the altar. Eventually dialogue forms developed, often between the celebrant and the deacon, or between the priest and some of the assembly. Some of these prayers were the same as the ones used at that time for sacramental absolution in the rites of reconciliation, yet the focus of the Penitential Rite is not individual sin, but our *communal* sense of unworthiness and *sinfulness in general*. This is more in line with the meaning of the Latin word *penitentia*. While this is closely associated with "doing penance" in our thinking, it actually means "change of heart." The Penitential Rite is concerned first with deepening our conversion.

There are four basic forms of the rite provided in the *Missal*. One option is the Rite of Blessing and Sprinkling Holy Water. This calls us to be mindful of our Baptism and to seek our ongoing cleansing and protection. It is especially suitable for Mass on Sunday and Mass in the season of Easter. This *asperges,* as the sprinkling is commonly known, recalls the power of our celebration of the Eucharist for our ongoing conversion and place in God's kingdom.

Three other, more directly confessional, ritual forms of the Pentitential Rite are also provided. They share a common desire for reflective silence. One is the *Confiteor.* This was one of the medieval private prayers of humility offered by the priest before saying Mass. The presider's invitations to the prayer direct us toward recognizing our failures and sins—but in light of God's pardon and compassion. A second form is based around a pair of psalm verses, one of which proclaims: "LORD, we have sinned against you" (cf. Ps 51:4), the other: "LORD, show us your mercy and love" (cf. Ps 85:7).

A third confessional ritual option—and perhaps the most extensively used one—combines penitential statements with the ancient *Kyrie eleison* (Lord, have mercy) litany. This option allows for a variety of ministers and attempts to respond to the particular situation of the community. It falls to the presider to invite the people to repentance and to pray the closing prayer for God's forgiveness. However, the invocations may be read or sung not just by the priest, but by the deacon or another suitable minister. Moreover, the invocations are not fixed: they may be improvised to suit particular occasions or assemblies. Of course, such improvisations ought to follow the general sense and style of those offered in the *Missal*.

Unfortunately, this third option has a feature that is somewhat unhelpful. In taking up the response from the *Kyrie eleison* (Lord, have mercy), we tend to think that *mercy* has the sense of forgiveness for our sins. In fact, as we will see, this is a misreading of the original sense of the prayer.

Kyrie Eleison: Lord, Have Mercy

First to its root meaning. The *Kyrie* is *not* essentially about our sinfulness and need for God's pardon. If that were so, we would kneel during its recitation, not stand. The *Kyrie* is a "standing" prayer whose deepest sense is *petition*. In it, we seek God's help, all the while praising God's mercy. Its sense is: *Lord, in your pity/mercy, grant us what we need....* While this might strike us as slightly odd, it is worth recalling that the *Kyrie* belongs to the family of prayers that fall under the category of litany. A review of the liturgical history of the *Kyrie* will add further insights.

For the first three centuries and longer, Greek—not Latin—was the preferred language of worship in Rome. By the mid-fifth century the liturgy was in Latin, including the readings and the Eucharistic Prayer. But the *Kyrie,* a Greek prayer, does not belong to this early period. It was added to the entrance rites well after Greek was a forgotten tongue in Rome! Nor was the *Kyrie* translated into Latin. What can this tell us?

The introduction of a Greek prayer into a thoroughly Latin liturgy signaled to the worshipers in the great cosmopolitan city of Rome that different cultures existed—not just the one culture. Romans alone did not constitute the "world"—an ever present tempting thought for the citizens of that once mighty center. But not only did the prayer remind the Romans that there were worlds and cultures outside their walls: it reminded them that these too belonged to God. Further, it had the potential to enable the assembly to accept Christians who were from different languages and cultures. The relevance of this should not be lost on us. Asian, African, European, Anglo, Celtic, Indian, Aboriginal—the *Kyrie* asks: Why do these differentiations mean so much to us when they mean nothing to God? In fact, they *obscure* God's ways. And if the way we live out divisions between groups is not to belong in the assembly, then should we not remove such prejudice from our society as well?

Whose words then are we echoing when we say the *Kyrie?* With whom do we stand? Now, the prayer is not only in Greek, it resonates with some New Testament passages. Mark's Gospel tells us of Bartimaeus (Mk 10:46–48). A blind beggar, Bartimaeus hears of Jesus passing by. He yells out: "Jesus, Son of David, have mercy on me!" When the *Kyrie* is said in Greek (the original language of the New Testament), our prayer echoes his petition. Matthew too gives us virtually the same plea ("Have mercy on us, Son of David!") in his recounting of the cure of two blind men (Mt 9:27). In both stories the essential ingredient is faith. Interestingly, Mark places his narrative with that of the rich man who has wealth but is blind to what Jesus has to offer (Mk 10:17–22). However, the blind and shunned Bartimaeus has insight into the power of Christ. In faith, he is cured and follows Jesus.

The most exact correspondence between the *Kyrie* and Scripture is found further on in Matthew. A Canaanite woman pleads with Jesus: "Have mercy on me, Lord, Son of David; my daughter is tormented by a demon" (Mt 15:22). Jesus refuses her request initially since she is a not from the House of Israel: she is a foreigner. But she persists in her request and her persistence pays off: while her name is lost to us, her faith is legendary. Remembering the cultural context of the meeting, her imposition on Jesus is rightly challenged. After all, she is a foreigner, and a woman. She has a daughter, not a son. The child is ill—a sign that the mother or the family has sinned. In the New Testament era, sickness is a moral problem. Yet it is her plea, her prayer, that we echo Sunday after Sunday at the Eucharist. We take up her words. Do we dare stand with her? Will we identify with her sufferings? In our own day, will we be brothers and sisters to the foreign workers, oppressed women, and the suffering parents of sick children in our midst?

The *Kyrie* is a stark reminder that in the assembly we are all foreigners, outsiders—all blind, all sinful. Nevertheless, we stand as adopted children of God our Father and give thanks. Such adoption is the gracious gift of God. All our relationships are built upon this divine generosity. Ours *is* the liturgy of the poor.

The *Gloria*

The *Gloria* is a song! In fact, it is the only *full* song in the entire Order of the Mass. Yes, we sing other parts in the Mass, but here we have a complete song, one sung simply for the glory and praise it expresses. What is more, as a song it belongs to the assembly as a whole. How did it find its way into the Mass?

Originally the *Gloria* was sung in the Liturgy of the Hours (the daily public prayer of the Church) as part of morning prayer. It was quite popular. As well, the opening verses, "Glory to God in the highest and peace to God's people on earth," recalled the praise of the angels in the story of their proclamation of the birth of Christ to the shepherds (Lk 2:14). Around the sixth century, the song was introduced into the Christmas Mass of the bishop. Its usage then slowly broadened to Eucharistic celebrations on Sundays, and feasts of a martyr, when the bishop was presiding. Some centuries later, the *Gloria* took up a place in any Mass on a Sunday or major feast. The exception, of course, was during Lent and Advent. As well, the *Gloria* remains in reserve ready to ring out on the nights of Holy Thursday, the Easter Vigil, and the Christmas Mass.

The *Gloria* is very much the song of the entire assembly: the *General Instruction* emphasizes that it belongs to the congregation as a whole, rather than to a choir or small group as a special, virtuoso piece. As well, the *Instruction* allows the *Gloria* to be introduced by various ministers—either the priest, the cantor, or the choir. The *Instruction* even puts forward different ways the hymn may be sung: by the people together, by the people alternately with the choir or, as a third option, by the choir alone. When the community is not able to sing this great act of praise, it is encouraged to recite it together or to have the assembly divide into two sections and recite the prayer alternating between sections (GIRM, no. 53).

The Opening Prayer or Collect

The Introductory Rites come to their climax with the Opening Prayer or collect. This is the most ancient prayer in these beginning rituals. It is a very interesting example of the way the liturgy responds to the cultures in which it is celebrated. As we saw above with the *Kyrie eleison,* the Christians of Rome used Greek in the liturgy roughly up until the middle of the fourth century. When they slowly moved to Latin, they realized that they could create new forms of prayers, forms suitable to the genius of this increasingly prominent language. One such product was the collect style of prayer. This style is common to our current Opening Prayer, the Prayer over the Gifts, and the Prayer after Communion. So popular did the collect style of prayer prove to be that thousands of them were written, copied, re-used, imported, modified, and passed down from generation to generation across Western Europe. Well-crafted versions of the prayer were characterized by brevity, depth, simplicity, and musical tone—features that have proven difficult to capture in translation from Latin.

The collect prayer has a particular shape. It begins with a call to prayer by the presider, followed by a period of silence. This silence should not be underplayed. It is a key moment in the prayer. During it, all those who have gathered silently, yet as one single body, place their needs and petitions before God.

When enough time has been given to this, the presider prays the written text. Almost without exception, this prayer is addressed to God, and concludes with a formula offering it through Christ in the Holy Spirit. According to the *General Instruction* the people make this spoken prayer their own with their acclamation, *Amen* (GIRM, no. 54).

With the Opening Prayer, the Introductory Rites come not only to a climax but also to a close. In a sense it both "collects" the silent petitions of the assembly and serves to complete the "collecting" of all the people present into a single body. With this final act of assembling, the assembly is now ready to hear the word of God.

Chapter 2
The Liturgy of the Word

Whenever, therefore, the Church,

> *gathered by the Holy Spirit for liturgical celebration,*

announces and proclaims the word of God,

it has the experience of being a new people

in whom the covenant made in the past is fulfilled.

(GIL, no. 7)

The Mass is made up, as it were, of two parts:

> *the Liturgy of the Word and the Liturgy of the Eucharist.*

These, however, are so closely interconnected

that they form but one single act of worship.

For in the Mass

> *the table both of God's word and of Christ's Body is prepared,*

from which the faithful may be instructed and refreshed.

(GIRM, no. 28)

In the description of the Mass from Justin Martyr that we saw earlier, we noted that the celebration has always had the reading of the Scriptures at its base. Through the inspiration and support of the Holy Spirit, however, the word of God becomes not only the foundation of the liturgical celebration but also the rule and support of every aspect of our lives (GIL, no. 9). The classic structure of this liturgical action, the Liturgy of the Word, comprises a series of set biblical readings, which are responded to by a homily and prayers of intercession. Our contemporary Mass however has also added the Creed to this ancient pattern.

The Second Vatican Council (the second assembly of the Catholic bishops of the world at the Vatican, held over four sessions between 1962 and 1965), has reminded us of a great liturgical truth, namely, that Christ is present in four different modes in the Eucharist. We enter into one of those modes with the proclamation of the Scriptures. No one has ever referred to this mode of Christ's presence better than that renowned Scripture scholar and translator, St. Jerome (c. 342–420):

> I think that the Gospel is the body of Christ and that the Holy Scriptures are his doctrine. When the Lord speaks about eating his flesh and drinking his blood certainly this can mean the mystery [of the Eucharist]. However, his true Body and Blood are [also] the Word of the Scriptures and its doctrine.[1]

Bearing in mind what St. Jerome has to say about the word of God, its proclamation can be seen to be one of the privileged moments in the Mass.

From here, we will consider some aspects common to the Scripture readings (the use of the ambo, the ritual form of the readings, and the ministry of reading), and then we will take up each of the Scripture passages and responses for the Sunday liturgy. Next, we will examine the liturgical books containing the readings—the *Lectionary* and the *Book of the Gospels*—along with some questions regarding silence, readings for children, and the weekday readings. Finally, I will comment on the homily, the Creed, and the general intercessions (the prayers of the faithful). The best guide to the Liturgy of the Word is the little-known *General Introduction to the Lectionary* (GIL). Published at the front of Volume One of the *Lectionary for Sundays,* it offers general principles for celebrations of the word of God and their incorporation into the Mass, and information about the order of readings for Mass. There are also very worthwhile relevant sections in the *Directory for Masses with Children* (DMC).

The Ambo

Scripture readings are central to the liturgy; their centrality is symbolized most clearly by the ambo or lectern. The ambo stands in the sanctuary alongside the altar and the presider's chair. It is the focal point for the Liturgy of the Word and, to be suitable for this task, it should be a substantial structure. Normally its use is restricted to the readings, the psalm, the *Exultet* at Easter, the homily, and the intercessions (GIRM, no. 309). The ambo is not a place of convenience for issuing directions or making community announcements but the place for proclamation of the word.

The Ritual Form of the Readings

Every Scripture reading is introduced, however, by an announcement! But this announcement is meant to get the attention of the hearers and to arouse their faith and curiosity. When the reader says, "A reading from the Prophet Isaiah," the hearers are invited to be alert to what this book might be calling them to be or do. The announcement itself presumes that the faithful will grow more and more familiar with the Scriptures throughout their lives, and so be at home with the book being read to them. Full, conscious, and active participation in the readings (see page 35) is accomplished through an intentional listening in silence. In this connection, the opening announcement also doubles as a call to silence. There seemed to be a need for such a call in former times: in an ancient liturgy from Syria, for example, the deacon ordered: "Sit down and be quiet." Nor were the citizens of Rome exempt from poor behavior: a command to catechumens (people receiving instruction in the faith) found in one of the Roman liturgical books was quite blunt: "Stand in silence and listen well." Our current rite also recommends a prayerful silence after the assembly has responded with thanks that the word of the Lord has been presented in its midst:

> At the end, the reader makes the acclamation, "The Word of the Lord," and all respond, "Thanks be to God." Then a few moments of silence may be observed as appropriate, so that all may briefly meditate on what they have heard (GIRM, no. 128; GIL, no. 28).

The Ministry of Reading

Who are qualified to be ministers of the first two Sunday Mass readings, that is, the Old Testament reading and the reading from the New Testament other than the Gospel? Since the aim of reading the word is that it be heard, the reader firstly must be someone who can read well. Poor reading is unacceptable. If the Scriptures cannot be heard then the whole point of reading them to the assembly is lost! It goes without saying here that a good sound system is a most important feature in a church. Yet more is required in proclaiming the word than a person who can read and use a good microphone. Because reading is a ministry, a reader must be, secondly, someone who prepares him or herself spiritually for the task. Effective proclamation of the word of God calls for vocal preparation of the reading, prayer with and over the text, and a spirituality of humble service. Ongoing training in reading and singing, along with continual study of the Scriptures, are indispensable. Reader, cantor, deacon, and priest alike may all proclaim the divine word, but none may take this ministry lightly.

The *General Instruction* insists, however, that all the readings, except the Gospel, be proclaimed by the laity. This ministry is viewed as an office in its own right, and is not to be co-opted by the ordained. Lay readers are to exercise their role even when ordained ministers are present (GIRM, no. 99). This is a first reminder that all the members of the assembly, ordained and lay alike, fall under the word of God.

The Old Testament Reading

The first of our set Sunday readings is from the Old Testament. Immediately, this makes us mindful of our Jewish heritage and of the way God has worked throughout history to bring the kingdom of grace. Many of the readings we hear were heard by Jesus himself. As he was formed, so we are formed. This connection with Jesus and the early Church is given further impetus through the arrangement of the Sunday Old Testament readings. They are included in the *Lectionary* because they contain a reference to the Gospel reading that will shortly follow. This is intended to bring out the unity of the two testaments, while still enabling texts of major significance to be read on Sundays. For pastoral reasons, these excerpts have been kept relatively short and easy to grasp.

Interestingly, for the Sundays of Easter and Pentecost Sunday, the first reading is not from the Old Testament but rather from the Acts of the Apostles.

The Psalm

The psalm has a number of interesting layers of meaning. As a psalm it is first a part of our Scriptures. We are a bit too quick to forget that it is the word of God! Moreover, it usually comes from the Book of Psalms, the great songbook of the people of Israel. Sometimes the liturgy makes use of the songs found in the other Old Testament books too. At its heart the psalm is a song, and like all songs, it cries out for music and singing.

Because the psalm is a song, active participation in this part of the Liturgy of the Word requires more than silent listening. Most attention is given to a responsorial form, with a cantor singing the verses and the whole congregation joining in a response. However, a second possibility is offered. The psalm can be sung all the way through either by the community as a whole or by a cantor, with the congregation listening attentively. According to the *General Introduction to the Lectionary,* singing most enhances the role and effect of the psalm: "The singing of the psalm, or even of the response alone, is a great help toward understanding and meditating on the psalm's spiritual meaning" (GIL, no. 21).

The psalm is considered so important that it is retained even when an assembly is unable to sing. However, in that case, it should be recited in such a way that it allows us to meditate on the word of God. It is very unfortunate when a community is able to sing other parts of the Mass, but not this scriptural song. The *General Introduction to the Lectionary* offers the broadest possible encouragement for promoting singing at this point in the Mass: "To foster the congregation's singing [the psalm], every means available in the various cultures is to be employed" (GIL, no. 21).

This part of the Mass had come to be known as the Gradual, but this term is no longer used. The name came from the Latin word for a step, *gradus,* since, at one stage, the psalm was sung from the steps of the ambo while only the Gospel was read from the top. Now the psalm is sung or recited from the lectern.

The New Testament Readings
Other Than the Gospels

The second Sunday reading, taken the various Letters of the New Testament, has not been chosen in connection with either the Gospel or the Old Testament passage.

Over a series of Sundays in Ordinary Time, successive selections from a single book have been set so that the assembly comes to hear key passages from that work. Because this way of ordering the readings does not include whole books from the Scriptures but only sequential selections from them, it is called "semi-continuous" reading. It is similar to what the first Christians did. During the Sunday Eucharist they would read from a scriptural book for as long as it was felt appropriate. Then, on the following Sunday, the next reader would pick up where the last had left off. This method of "continuous" reading was subsequently adapted for our contemporary usage. However, during the major seasons (Advent, Christmas, Lent and Easter) and on solemnities, the second set reading from the New Testament (other than the Gospels) matches the theme of the particular liturgy.

The Gospel Acclamation

We greet the Gospel with cries of *Alleluia*—except during Lent, when they are replaced by another chant. The term "Alleluia" is actually a Hebrew word meaning "Praise God." It joyfully resounds at the very close of the Book of Psalms, in the final verses of the final song: "Let everything that breathes praise the LORD! Praise the LORD!" (Ps 150:6).

The chant welcoming the Gospel serves not only to greet the Gospel, rousing all to stand and welcome the Lord who is about to speak to them: it also accompanies any procession of the *Book of the Gospels*. This occurs especially when the *Book of the Gospels* has been placed on the altar during the entrance procession, and is subsequently carried aloft to the ambo.

Since the *Alleluia* is a chant, should it not be sung? Clearly, the intention of the liturgical instructions is "yes," it should be sung. Moreover, all are to stand and sing the *Alleluia,* led by the choir or a cantor (GIRM, no. 62). Furthermore, it is a song in which the whole community has a key part, though verses may be sung by a cantor or choir. According to the *General Instruction of the Roman Missal,* on those occasions when there is only one reading before the Gospel—such as many weekdays, but also possibly on Sundays—the chant may be omitted if it is not sung (no. 63c). The norm then is that the *Alleluia* be sung.

The Gospel

The Roman liturgy—which we celebrate in a contemporary form—has put great energy and creativity into the proclamation of the Gospel. The Gospel reading has a special minister, is accompanied by the *Alleluia,* and has its own greetings. And, significantly, during its proclamation, the entire assembly stands. The reader reverences the script with a kiss. The rite may also be enhanced with incense and lights (e.g., lighted candles). There may even be a *Book of the Gospels*—a separate, ornately decorated book containing only the Gospel passages—which is carried in procession to the ambo.

We begin the Gospel reading with a call to prayer:

Ordained Minister: The Lord be with you.

Assembly: And also with you.

The reading is then opened with an acclamation—

Ordained Minister: A reading from the Holy Gospel according to [John].

Assembly: Glory to you, O Lord.

which will be mirrored by a closing one:

Ordained Minister: The Gospel of the Lord.

Assembly: Praise to you, Lord Jesus Christ.

In these short verses the assembly praises Christ who is present in the readings. These ritual acclamations heighten our awareness of the power and mystery of God at work during their proclamation. The one who proclaims the Gospel also kisses the *Book of the Gospels*. This is the second kiss in the liturgy. Each kiss signifies something of the way Christ is present in our worship. At the beginning of Mass the altar is kissed, and now the book containing the Gospel passage is kissed.

The set selections from the Gospels for the Sundays of Ordinary Time are "semi-continuous." There is a three-year cycle in which a year is given over to Matthew (Year A), Mark (Year B), and Luke (Year C). This allows the assembly to hear the life and preaching of Jesus as presented by each of the sacred authors. For the other seasons, and on solemnities, the Gospel is related to the distinctive theme that is celebrated. In this connection, the Gospel of John is especially prominent during the seven weeks of Easter.

The Minister of the Gospel

Who should read the Gospel? The answer may not be as obvious as we think! Most of us are used to the priest proclaiming this reading. Indeed many priests and others think it is his role. However that is not quite the case. The reading of the Gospel belongs to the deacon. A couple of points need to be drawn from this. Firstly, it is a powerful reminder that all the assembly—faithful, presider, bishop, concelebrants— all of us together, fall under the word of God. Secondly, it is something of a wake-up call for us. The Sunday liturgy presumes the presence of a deacon. Yet the experience of the vast majority of us is that the Mass is celebrated without one. There is something essential missing from the Church when one of its key hierarchical levels (bishop, priest, deacon) is absent from our experience. In effect, it can mean that the role of the presider is expanded beyond its proper horizons. If there is no deacon, who then should read? The *General Instruction* gives an interesting answer to this question, detailing that the proclamation should fall to a priest other than the presider. Only when there is neither a deacon nor another concelebrating priest should the presiding celebrant announce the

Gospel (GIRM, no. 59). In effect, the presider is to read the Gospel by exception. But when the exception becomes the norm, a distortion can creep into our liturgical thinking and celebrating!

The Posture for Hearing the Gospel

While we sit for the first two readings and the psalm, we stand for the Gospel. This variation in posture dates back to at least the fourth century. Here we will turn directly to the work of liturgist Joseph Jungmann, one of the giants in the study of liturgy in the twentieth century. His research on the history and pastoral nature of the liturgy of the Mass is the standard reference. In the following extract, he describes how former generations of the faithful stood for the Gospel, and the meanings they gave this posture:

> When the deacon's greetings sound all stand up and turn to him. Thereupon all the peoples face east, till the words of our Lord begin. Meanwhile the canes that are used to support oneself are put aside and the people either stand erect (like servants before their Lord) or else slightly bowed. The men are to remove every head covering, even the princely crown. Mention is made, too, of setting aside one's weapons and outer mantle or cloak, as well as gloves. Elsewhere the knights laid their hand on the hilt of their sword, or they drew the sword and held it extended all during the reading—expressions, both, of a willingness to fight for the word of God.[2]

We stand *under* the Gospel, humble servants in the presence of Christ, listening to his word and readying ourselves to do his will.

Silence

The Liturgy of the Word also needs silence (GIRM, no. 56; GIL, no. 28). Silence acts in concert with listening, reading, singing, acclamation, standing, kissing, and the many other actions and events in the rite. Moments of silence enable the assembly to become meditative, take the word of God to heart, and respond in prayer. Hence, short intervals of quiet are recommended after the readings and the homily. Any overt busyness or haste works against the atmosphere of recollection so necessary for fruitful listening. Our attentive silence gives the Spirit room to move.

The *Lectionary* and the *Book of the Gospels*

The book that holds in order all the readings for the Sunday Mass, as well as those for weekdays and feasts, is known as the *Lectionary*. The title comes from the Latin word for a reading: *lectio*. The *Book of the Gospels,* similarly, contains the Gospel passages in order. These ritual books give prominence and dignity to the word of God. As well, compared to using a Bible, they make it easy to find the readings for each day and feast. They contain the version of the Scriptures approved for liturgical use in any one particular country. At times, the different conferences of bishops (bishops considered collectively, according to country) in the English-speaking world have authorized that the *Lectionary* use a specific translation.

Does this mean that no other version of the Scriptures may be used in the liturgy? Not quite. Any particular conference of bishops may also approve other translations for use in the liturgy, even though it does not wish them to become the basis of the *Lectionary*. The result is that alternative translations may be used when pastorally helpful. Such potential to use various Scripture versions is crucial. The whole point of providing such options is that nothing should stand in the way of hearing the word of God. Official approval of course is required to ensure that what is heard is both a faithful translation and a liturgically appropriate reading: not every translation is accurate enough or suitable for proclamation in the liturgy.

In the medieval Church, the *Book of the Gospels* was often a wondrous thing. There are copies on parchment or calf skin, dyed royal purple and written on in lettering of gold. The *Book of Kells* is justly famous for its artwork and lettering. Today we require texts that are easier to use and at the same time worthy for use in our worship. However, it is ironic when we give more attention to the "book" than to the "word" it contains! The exquisite copies from the Middle Ages are breathtaking. But the readings they contain were proclaimed in Latin, a language that the vast majority of the faithful had long ceased to understand. What is the point of a beautiful book if the readings it contains are unintelligible?

The fourth-century desert monks knew something of the dilemma of putting too much value on the book and not enough on our own conversion:

> One of the monks, called Serapion, sold his *Book of the Gospels* and gave the money to those who were hungry, saying: I have sold the book which told me to sell all that I had and give to the poor.[3]

The *Weekday Lectionary*

A separate *Lectionary* comprises the weekday readings. Two readings and a psalm are set down for each Mass. For Ordinary Time, the first readings have been chosen from various books in either the Old or the New Testament. They are set out in a two-year cycle. Each book is read semi-continuously over several days or weeks. The Gospels are arranged into a single sequence, repeated yearly. Mark is read first, followed by Matthew. The year closes with Luke. It is only ever by accident that the two readings at a weekday Mass have themes in common. The intention underlying the selection of readings however has not been to set apparently divergent readings together but to open up to the faithful as wide a selection of the word of God as possible. Unlike the readings for

Ordinary Time though, there is more convergence between the first and Gospel readings for the various seasons, as well as for solemnities and feasts.

Masses with Children

It is worth turning to the *Directory for Masses with Children* to see what it says about children and the celebration of the word. The *Directory* is concerned that children could be neglected in the usual Sunday liturgy. Consequently it recommends that parts of the introduction to the Mass of the day and the homily be addressed directly to them. A separate celebration of the Liturgy of the Word, homily included, is offered as a way to do this.

More is said in the *Directory* about Masses where children are in the majority. These junior members of the faithful are encouraged to be cantors or readers, to respond when a homily is given in dialogue form, and to recite the intentions of the prayers of the faithful (DMC, no. 22). Every effort should be made so that the spiritual wealth of the readings is opened up to the young. This may include changing the set readings, adapting particular passages, choosing a more suitable translation, and even having the children read the text in parts (DMC, nos. 41–9). There is provision for an adult to speak to the children after the readings if the presider himself does not feel confident that he can reach the hearers at their level.

While the *Directory* deals specifically with children, it expresses a primary concern for the Liturgy of the Word. Again, if no one can make sense of the readings when they are read, either because readers read poorly, microphones are inadequate, or there is too much ceremony and movement, then the whole point of that part of the Mass is lost! The word is meant to be heard.

The Homily

The homily is one of the most ancient parts of the Sunday Mass. It is the prime place in the liturgy where the needs and lives of the hearers are brought into direct dialogue with the readings just heard and the mystery being celebrated that day. The homily, because it is within the Eucharist itself, should lead the community to celebrate the Mass wholeheartedly.

Our word "homily" has its origins in the Greek word for a conversation. Homilies are meant to have a level of informality. This suits their purpose of breaking open the word of God so that it can nourish the flesh-and-blood lives of the faithful (GIRM, no. 65). The *General Instruction* points out that the homily should be based on the readings or another text used in the same liturgy. It is not an opportunity for grand rhetoric and fulsome prose. Nor is it primarily a moment for handing across teachings, though occasionally it can have this role. Not only should the content be relevant and at the level of the hearers, so should the delivery be at their level. When the homily is too long or too wordy or too distant, then a disservice is done to the word of God.

The homily is a liturgical act as well. Occasionally though the inappropriate timing of pious practices can cause confusion in this part of the ritual. Some homilists, for example, invite the faithful to bless themselves before or after the homily, or to address them with a salutation such as "Praised be Jesus Christ," practices that have their origin in preaching outside Mass. Such practices are discouraged since the homily is part of the actual liturgy itself, and the assembly has already blessed itself and been greeted at the beginning of Mass.

Who can give the homily? Throughout the centuries the homily at Mass has usually been preached by the presider. This highlights the close link between the actual celebration taking place and the pastoral leadership of the community. The presider may invite another ordained minister—priest or deacon—to deliver the homily. This preserves the authoritative, pastoral heart and the liturgical form of the ritual action.

However, as always throughout the Mass, pastoral concerns and opportunities should be given consideration. Where prudent, the homilist may engage the assembly in a "dialogue" homily in which he invites responses from the assembly. Other forms of preaching that supplement the regular homily are also allowed. We have already seen that the *Directory for Masses with Children* has a provision for the presider to allow an adult to speak to the children after the Gospel if he finds it difficult to adapt himself to the mentality of the children (DMC, no. 24). Other forms of instruction and personal testimonies may also have a place. This is said most clearly in the relevant document itself:

> A form of instruction designed to promote a greater understanding of the liturgy, including personal testimonies, or the celebration of Eucharistic liturgies on special occasions (e.g., day of the seminary, day of the sick, etc.) is lawful, if in harmony with liturgical norms, should such be considered objectively opportune as a means of explicating the regular homily preached by the celebrant priest. Nonetheless, these testimonies or explanations may not be such so as to assume a character which could be confused with the homily.[4]

The Creed

Our present Roman liturgy prays the Creed in the Mass on Sundays and solemnities. But it was not always so! The Creed originates in the sacrament of Baptism: the Apostles' Creed was a baptismal creed in Rome. The earliest version of the Nicene Creed is encountered as an ancient Jerusalem baptismal creed. It later developed into approximately the form we now have as a symbol of the beliefs proclaimed at two early Christian Councils, namely, the Councils of

Nicea (325) and of Constantinople (381). How then did the Creed—a prayer that belongs in Baptism—find its way into the Mass?

First, we have to turn to the Eastern Church, and especially to the city of Constantinople. When Patriarch Timotheus (511–517) was accused of not having beliefs that were completely orthodox, he needed a defense. His answer was to show his zeal for the truth by including the Nicene Creed in the Mass! It was a bold and original move, soon copied by other Churches in the East. The Creed—also called the *symbol of faith*—was prayed by the assembly in conjunction with the sign of peace, which took place at the time of the presentation of gifts.

The Church in Rome did not copy this innovation, but in Spain it was another matter. There, in 589, King Reccared rejected Arianism (a fourth-century heresy maintaining that Jesus was not divine) and fully accepted the belief that Jesus was indeed divine. Consequently he ordered that the people make the Profession of Faith at Mass, just before the Our Father. The custom slowly spread. However, as chance would have it, the recitation of the Creed was introduced by Charlemagne (742–814) into his chapel at Aachen (Germany). He had it sung after the Gospel. Again it was not received with any great gusto throughout France. However, the recitation of the Creed became the common usage for the rulers who lived in Aachen. Subsequently, when Emperor Henry

II left that city to go to Rome in 1014, he was surprised that Rome did not follow his custom. The Roman priests responded that as the city had never known heresy, there was no need to recite the Creed at every Sunday Mass! Nevertheless the Emperor had his way and Pope Benedict VIII (d. 1024) ordered that the symbol of faith be recited on Sundays and on the feasts that are mentioned in its text, that is, Christmas, Easter, Ascension, and Pentecost.

The Profession of Faith or Creed is now securely settled as a part of the Liturgy of the Word. It is a prayer of the entire assembly, fitting for Sundays and solemnities. While it may be led either by the priest, a cantor, or the choir, such ministers should not appear to take over the assembly when it is proclaimed. The *General Instruction* is clear about this. It allows for the Creed to be sung either by all simultaneously or by the people alternating in two groups or, if it is not sung, it recommends that the Creed be said by all or by the people alternating in two groups (GIRM, no. 68). The option to recite the Creed in parts, however, has not been exercised much to date.

The General Intercessions

The Prayer of the Faithful, or the general intercessions, should be counted among the most important prayers in the liturgy. At Baptism we become members of the priestly people of God (1 Pet 2:5). And as the priestly people, our function is to offer petitions to God for the salvation of all (GIRM, no. 69). So seriously did the early Church take the priestly baptismal significance of these prayers that before offering them, they dismissed from the assembly anyone who was not yet baptized. Here, then, we have one of the highest expressions in the Mass of the royal priesthood of the faithful.

Unfortunately, the history of the Prayer of the Faithful has not matched their significance. Toward the end of the sixth century in Rome, they lost popularity. There were too many other litany-style prayers like the general intercessions already included in the Mass. As well, these intercessions became overly repetitious and stylized. Poor practice meant that their importance was obscured, and they subsequently lost ground to newer forms of prayer.

The Prayer of the Faithful, however, is a most concrete expression of our faith. These prayers show our belief in God's love for us as God's adopted children: God wants to hear our prayers. The general intercessions constantly impress on us that our prayers are formed in the Spirit and heard through Christ, the High Priest. They also challenge us—as the embodiment of God's kingdom—to be mindful of the needs of all creation.

This theological significance is reflected in the rubrics, that is, the official directions laid down for the rite. The *General Instruction* admonishes us to include the general intercessions in all Masses (GIRM, no. 69), and because they are the prayer of the Church as a whole, though offered by individual local assemblies, a particular sequence of intentions is specified. Clearly this is modified when the liturgy reflects a particular celebration such as Confirmation or a funeral. The normal order of intentions is as follows:

1. For the needs of the Church;

2. For public authorities and the salvation of the whole world;

3. For those burdened by any kind of difficulty;

4. For the local community (GIRM, no. 70).

This ordering reminds the assembly that they pray for all God's world! This is what it means to offer prayers as the priestly people. The prayers should be especially concerned with peoples, places and incidents that are forgotten or given little attention. After all, if we do not pray for them, who will? This worldwide nature of the intercessions serves to remind us that we are not an insular, inward-looking body only concerned about our own welfare. We are deeply aware of our leaders, of the frailty of the Church, and of the poor and abandoned in the entire human community. It is only toward the end of the petitions that we turn our attention to our own needs. To share in the priesthood of Christ is to be steeped in the needs of the world, with eyes open to see, ears cocked to hear, and hearts ready to respond.

Who should lead the prayers? The role of the priest is limited. His part is to invite the faithful to pray and, later, to conclude the petitions with a brief prayer. The intentions are to be announced by a deacon, a cantor, a reader, or another member of the assembly. The prayers become the prayer of the community through the invocation ("Lord, hear our prayer") or the petitions made in silence at the end of each intention. These two features—the silence and the invocation—are the very heart of the prayer. They deserve every attention!

Who should write the prayers? There are no books of intercessions that we are bound to follow. The liturgy simply requires that the petitions have the following characteristics. They should be well considered prayers, succinct and freely but discreetly composed, and they should express the prayer of the entire community (GIRM, no. 71). Here is a great opportunity for the involvement of various members of a parish in the creation of the liturgy.

With the short concluding prayer, the presider brings the general intercessions to a close and signals the end of the Liturgy of the Word.

Chapter 3

The Preparation of the Gifts

THE RITES THAT MAKE UP THE Preparation of the Gifts
have a simple and single aim. Through them the faithful
bring their gifts of bread and wine to the altar as a prel-
ude to the great thanksgiving prayer of blessing: they
make up one of the moments of the Mass which clearly
show the priestly nature of the people of God. The
bread and the wine are our bread and our wine—or at
least in the past, they came from the tables, kitchens, and
cellars of the faithful. Yet they are only bread and only
wine. Nothing else. And they have only one purpose.
The bread is to be eaten, the wine to be drunk. By the
action of God, what we bring to the table will be transformed and given back to us from the table. Nothing
else is brought up during the Preparation of the Gifts
unless it is for the hunger and thirst of the poor or for
the needs of the Church as the body of Christ.

The Bread and the Wine

At the Last Supper, Jesus taught us to remember
him in the breaking of the blessed bread and the shar-

ing of the blessed cup. In the early Christian centuries, each member of the assembly, or perhaps each family, brought along to Mass a loaf of bread and a flask of wine. Homemade breads took different shapes. Sometimes they were round, or had a braid on top, or were in the form of a crown. However, by the ninth century a new practice emerged in the Western Church. The bread was no longer leavened but unleavened. This became the rule during the eleventh century. Soon after, in the twelfth century, the now familiar small hosts, round like coins, made their appearance.

The wine that was brought from the homes of the faithful was usually red. This stayed the custom, more or less. However there was no rigid regulation. In the sixteenth century, the use of white wine became more common. By then, white purificators had been introduced to clean the chalice after Communion. Since white wine stained the linen less than the red, the sacristan would order the color that made for less work.

Because the wine produced by the ancients was so strong, it was always prepared with water before being served. Sometimes the mix was one part wine to two parts water. Our mixing of some water with the wine comes from this practice.

Different countries and cities had different customs for bringing the gifts from the faithful to the altar. A custom in Rome at the Mass celebrated by the pope was for him, other bishops and clergy, to go to the people and bring forth from them their bread and wine. Rome, being a deeply hierarchical society, ordered this gathering accordingly. The pope received from the highest aristocrats, the bishops from the upper levels of society, and the priests and deacons from the rest (in the back area of the church). When all the wine had been collected and the breads laid on the altar, the master of ceremonies set aside enough for Communion for all present. The rest was put into storage where it was kept for the poor and the upkeep of the clergy. A different custom was followed in Gaul (France). There, the deacon met the people at the door and placed their gifts in the sacristy. He would place on the altar only what was required for Communion, setting aside the remainder for the poor and the clergy.

Our reformed liturgy has tried to retrieve some of the riches of the past, but has not fully succeeded. The procession aims to highlight the priestly nature of the assembly, and to give prominence to their gifts. This is also a suitable time for a collection and the presentation of gifts for the poor. Yet the bread brought to the altar rarely resembles a common loaf of bread, and only in some places is the cup commonly offered. The *General Instruction* actually reflects some confusion over the bread. On the one hand, it sets out that the bread be unleavened and baked in the "traditional" shape. On the other, it wants the bread to appear as food, commenting that the nourishing nature of the consecrated bread demands that what we use at Mass actually appear to be food (GIRM, no. 321). We still have some way to go before we can feel again the homely significance of the loaf and the cup.

How much bread and wine should be brought up? The answer is quite clear: enough for Communion for all, as well as some for the absent sick, and enough for the dying. We should also receive Communion from the bread consecrated at the same Mass (GIRM, no. 85).

The Procession

There is a tendency to misunderstand the ritual of the presentation of the gifts. It is not an explicit offering of our lives, achievements, or prayers. Such an understanding springs from giving too much attention to the former name for the rite, the offertory. Rather we have here an act of preparation. We cannot go on to the prayer of thanksgiving unless our bread and wine are on the altar. They are the focus of the procession—along with any gifts for the good of the poor and the life of the Church. The bread and wine are placed on the altar, the alms and collection nearby. The procession of the gifts ought to be accompanied by a song, which should continue at least till the gifts are placed on the altar, but should not prolong the rite (GIRM, no. 74).

Once the bread and wine have been placed on the altar, there is an option to incense the gifts, the cross, and the altar. Here we have an action symbolising that these three are all connected in the thanksgiving prayer we are about to offer God. The deacon or another minister may also incense all present, a reminder of the dignity we have from Baptism and which we exercise through our various ministries (GIRM, no. 75).

The Blessing Prayers

In the current liturgy we have two quite beautiful prayers of blessing. They come from the Jewish tradition of prayers at the meal table. In them we bless God because all we have and do is from God. We also name the bread and wine as our gifts, the work of our hands from the fruit of God's providence. Finally, we praise God because of the divine action that will make them our spiritual nourishment. These prayers can be said silently or out loud. If the song or music has not yet ended the two simple blessings are said in silence.

Following these blessings is a selection of prayers for the presider alone, for his spiritual preparation. As with all private prayers, they should not interfere with the communal prayer of the liturgy.

The Prayer over the Gifts

The Preparation of the Gifts ends with a prayer by the presider—a presidential prayer—over the gifts. Being a succinct, collect-style prayer, it is similar to the Opening Prayer of the Mass and the Prayer after Communion. It has commonly been known as the "Secret," though no one is quite sure why this is so. One theory is that the prayer came to be said in silence, with *secreta* referring to this quiet recitation. Another approach is that this came about because the presider prayed it over the gifts that had been "set apart" for the prayer of thanksgiving: the Latin word *secreta* comes from the verb *secernere,* to set apart.

With the conclusion of the Prayer over the Gifts, we are now ready for the most significant prayer of the Mass: the Eucharistic Prayer.

Chapter 4
The Eucharistic Prayer

THE EUCHARISTIC PRAYER COMPRISES several parts but, before turning to them, we need to ask what lies at the heart of the prayer. There are four things to keep in mind.

Our attention is most often first drawn to the profound teaching that it is in and through this prayer that the bread and wine are transformed into the Body and Blood of Christ. This accounts for the great reverence, devotion, and piety we have attached to this part of the liturgy. It also draws us into the mystery of Christ at the Last Supper, his subsequent betrayal to death, and the resurrection.

The next point is just as important. The Eucharistic Prayer is first and foremost, through and through, a prayer of thanksgiving. "Eucharist" comes from the Greek word for thanksgiving. The purpose at the center of every Eucharistic Prayer is to give thanks to God for all that has been accomplished for us in the life, death, and resurrection of Jesus, and the sending

of the Spirit. In a sense, the prayer is a public proclamation of our baptismal faith. We give thanks and
praise to the triune God without reservation because
in Christ we have been saved, and indeed all creation
has been made new! Yet there is more to the prayer.
Our praise and thanksgiving to God is made in Christ
himself. It is not just our individual wishes, but an act
of the body of Christ through Christ, the Head of his
body. These are the reasons why the prayer is held as
the center and summit of the entire celebration.

What does this mean for us? We give thanks for
the transformation God has wrought in our lives and
in our world. This is the recreation symbolized in our
Baptism. Each Sunday we reaffirm this and allow it to
reaffirm us, challenge us, confront us, comfort us.
This is not easy, but it is a brave act of hope against the
tragedy and despair that too often beset our lives, our
cities and towns, our lands. In the Eucharist we give
thanks to God for our hope, though it may be likened
to only a fragile taper of light. We lament our grief
too, as Christian thanksgiving involves naming not
just the good, but also the bad. Unless we offer this
thanksgiving, what sense can our faith have?

Thirdly, it is important for us to realize that the
liturgy of the Mass as a whole leads to this prayer. Our
conscious and active participation in the prayer flows
from our participation in all the preceding parts of the
liturgy. We tend though understand the Mass as
divided into discrete pieces. Recall the quote from the

General Instruction that we receive instruction and food from the table of God's word *and* of Christ's Body (GIRM, no. 28). No matter what our role in the liturgy may be—presider, deacon, concelebrant, or member of the assembly in general—our engagement in the Eucharistic Prayer is deficient unless we participate fully in the preceding rites of gathering and the word.

Finally, we need to understand clearly that the endpoint of the blessing prayer is our communion in the Body and Blood of the Lord. The pinnacle of the entire Eucharistic celebration is to enter into communion with Christ and with each other. Through Communion we are transformed into a single body, Christ's body. We show forth the kingdom of God, and experience a foretaste of the eternal banquet.

One of the challenges we face in the Eucharistic Prayer is to pray it fully, consciously, and actively. While each Eucharistic Prayer contains many of the same parts and follows much the same pattern, enabling us to become familiar with them quite easily, this can also mean that we let our attention wander. To offset this, there is provision for variation. Such variation prevents the prayers from being too bound down, thus helping them to "live."

We will consider the variations among the different Eucharistic Prayers at the end of this chapter. But before doing this, it will be worthwhile to consider their common components.

The Introductory Dialogue: "The Lord be with you...."

The introductory dialogue leads the Eucharistic Prayer. Our earliest record of its use dates from the early 200s. It is one of the most ancient, and stable, features of Eucharistic praying. Its simplicity and brevity belie its significance. It announces the prayer as one of thanksgiving prayed by the entire community together:

> *Presider:* Let us give thanks to the Lord our God.
> *Assembly:* It is right to give him thanks and praise.[1]

The exchange between presider and all others present is designed to rouse the whole assembly, focus their hearts and minds, and bring to mind the great acts of God. While all pray the prayer, the form of the text gives specific roles to particular ministers. This has been an unchanging feature from the very earliest prayers we know about. Remember how Justin Martyr described the prayer as one led by the presider.

The Preface

In relation to the preface, unfortunately, history, translation, and terminology have conspired to mislead us! For a time it was common to think that the Eucharistic Prayer did not begin until after the end of the Holy, Holy, Holy. It seemed as though the preface was something like the preface to a book, a sort of introductory piece. Of course the Latin term, *praefatio,* is close to "preface." However, the reality is quite different. The preface is the *first* great acclamation of our praise and thanksgiving to God. Its aim is to surprise us with, even wake us up to, the things that God has done.

Said by the presider, the preface has many variations and options. These allow the president to name the reasons for this particular thanksgiving celebration. The preface is chosen according to the liturgical occasion: Sunday, weekday Mass, season, or feast. Prefaces may also be chosen to reflect the pastoral situation of a funeral or marriage, or the Church's celebration of an ordination, or the dedication of a church building. Prefaces have been provided for a large number of needs and occasions. While this may seem a bit extravagant, it is worth knowing that the earliest liturgical collections we have from the ancient liturgy of Rome contain hundreds and hundreds of prefaces, often a new one for each Mass. What mattered was that every preface be appropriate and good. Through this prayer the presider leads the assembly to give thanks to God. In response, roused to action, we burst into song with the *Sanctus*.

The Sanctus: "Holy, Holy, Holy..."

The *Sanctus* is a song of the assembly. And although it may be said, it is at its best when sung. While it is not clear when the *Sanctus* was first used in the liturgy, it does seem to have had a place among the prayers of early second-century Christians in Rome.

The words are a compendium of different scriptural verses and references. The two most prominent verses are from Isaiah and Matthew: "Holy, holy, holy is the LORD of hosts; the whole earth is full of his glory" (Is 6:3); "Hosanna to the Son of David! Blessed is the one who comes in the name of the Lord! Hosanna in the highest heaven!" (Mt 21:9).

At the *Sanctus* we are invited to join our acclamation with the praise of heaven itself.

The Mighty Acts of God

With the *Sanctus* still resounding in our hearts, the presider leads us to consider the great acts of God. In particular we are brought to the narrative of the final meal of Jesus. This meal has become the center point of our praise. Through it we contemplate the great mystery of our redemption through Jesus' death and resurrection. We are aware of the central teaching of our faith that in the blessing of the loaf and cup through the words of consecration, Jesus becomes present in the sacrament of his Body and Blood. Implicit in this sacrament of the consecrated bread and wine is the command to eat and drink of the Body and Blood of Christ. Through this eating and drinking we enter into the most profound communion with Christ. In Communion, Jesus fulfills one of his most treasured promises, given to us in the Gospel of John: "Those who eat my flesh and drink my blood abide in me, and I in them" (6:56). In response to the mystery of redemption, we are moved again to acclaim the mystery of our faith.

The Memorial Prayer

At this point, the Eucharistic Prayer displays its ancient Jewish heritage by "remembering" the saving actions of God. One of the great Old Testament examples of "remembering" is the passage detailing what is to be said at Passover. One version reads as follows:

> When your children ask you in time to come, "What is the meaning of the decrees and the statutes and the ordinances that the LORD our God has commanded you?" then you shall say to your children, "We were Pharaoh's slaves in Egypt, but the LORD brought us out of Egypt with a mighty hand. The LORD displayed before our eyes great and awesome signs and wonders against Egypt, against Pharaoh and all his household. He brought us out from there in order to bring us in, to give us the land that he promised on oath to our ancestors. Then the LORD commanded us to observe all these statutes, to fear the LORD our God, for our lasting good...." (Deut 6:20–24).

The sense of this memorial prayer is that by calling to memory what God once did, the faithful are assured that God will continue to act in the present. Notice that when the passage refers to their ancestors and actions of God in the past, it uses the *first person* plural, for example: "The LORD brought *us* out of Egypt." The things that happened to their forebears are seen as having happened to those who are now present many generations later. At the same time God, too, is "reminded" to remain constant! In the Eucharistic Prayer, the Christian community is similarly called to keep memorial of *Christ* by recalling especially his passion and death, resurrection and ascension. This is a profound moment since it is through the paschal mystery of Christ that we are saved and given hope and strength in the present, and, in it too, all things are made new.

The Petition for the Spirit

Our contemporary prayers often have two separate invocations calling on the Spirit. Yet these two parts remain a single action. The Spirit is called upon both to hallow the gifts and to transform those present into the body of Christ. The Third Eucharistic Prayer expresses this pair of invocations as follows: "And so, Father, we bring you these gifts. We ask you to make them holy by the power of your Spirit, that they may become the Body and Blood of your Son..." and, "Grant that we, who are nourished by his Body and Blood, may be filled with his Holy Spirit, and become one body, one spirit in Christ."

Petitions for the Church and the Kingdom

Petitions for the pope and the local bishop convey a sense of immediacy. They convey that our Church and our assemblies are grounded in particular human beings. The petition for the pope is a reminder of the unity of the Church. Our prayer for the local bishop symbolizes his unique role in the very manifestation of the Church in this time and place. It is difficult to pray effectively for the pope and the local bishop unless we realize that they are simply men, very human servants of God, in need of our prayers.

The saints may well belong to the heavenly sphere, but their place in the Eucharistic Prayer is not without significance for our earthly concerns. They are seen both as intercessors on our behalf and as exemplars of the Christian life whose company we wish to enter. They also symbolize hopes, relationships, and needs in communities and, as such, their naming can be quite potent. An example centers around St. Joseph. He was invoked by Pope John XXIII as patron of the Second Vatican Council. Subsequently, the pontiff added his name to the list of saints in the Roman Canon (Eucharistic Prayer I). Consequently, to pray his name in the prayer is to take up something of the spirit and direction of the Council.

Government officials in the People's Republic of China protested the Vatican decision to canonize 120 Chinese martyrs on October 1, 2000. While they died before the end of 1930, the date chosen for their feast is the anniversary of Mao Zedong's more recent foundation of the People's Republic. Whether deliberate or accidental, every commemoration of those martyrs will bear an implicit critique of the Republic.

Across the Church, various dioceses, countries, religious orders, towns, villages, industries, professions, and the like have their own "proper" saints. Their particular significance and local flavor is brought to Eucharistic praying either when they are named in the Eucharistic Prayer, or even when general reference is made to the Communion of Saints. In this part of the prayer, our unity with Christ in the Spirit opens onto our union with the saints.

In conjunction with the saints we pray for the dead. Some Eucharistic Prayers give an opportunity to name particular people out loud, while every prayer allows us to pray silently on behalf of our dead. We pray for those we love and miss. Yet, as Christians offering the priestly prayer of Christ, we can expand our horizons. Should we not also use this moment to pray for those dead who have no one to pray for them? The nameless victims of violence, of injustice, of natural disasters all have a place in our hearts because, as the priestly people of God, our hearts are as broad and compassionate as the heart of God.

The Doxology

The Eucharistic Prayer ends the same way it began: with praise. Doxology means literally "words of praise" from the Greek *logos* (word) and *doxa* (praise). We respond joyfully with the *Amen*. Unfortunately, all too often the Great *Amen* is a thin and weak *amen!* Nevertheless, this cry brings the whole prayer to its conclusion. By our *Amen* we signify that we are at one with all that has been prayed. There is evidence from the early 700s of the presider and deacon raising the blessed bread and cup during the doxology. This elevation is one of the most poignant gestures in the whole prayer. Symbolically, we raise to God our praise, the work of our hands, the products of creation. We know we have all things through God, even this very prayer, and we give glory to Father, Son, and Spirit. We now prepare ourselves to be nourished by the fruits of God's action.

The Options Among the Eucharistic Prayers

There are many Eucharistic Prayers available for our celebrations. As with the other options in the liturgy, we are invited to choose those texts that will benefit the spiritual and pastoral needs of the particular assembly. The liturgy documents provide us with some guidance about which option to choose and when (GIRM, no. 365).

Eucharistic Prayer I (The Roman Canon)

The Roman Canon has inserts especially for the following feasts and seasons: Christmas, Epiphany, the Easter Vigil till the Second Sunday of Easter, Ascension, and Pentecost. It is also appropriate for the feasts of the Apostles and of the ancient Roman saints listed in the prayer, for example, Saints Cosmos and Damian.

Eucharistic Prayer II

This prayer is suitable for weekdays and special circumstances. It is also a good choice for Masses celebrated for someone who has died.

Eucharistic Prayer III

Eucharistic Prayer III is described as particularly suited to Sundays and major feasts.

Eucharistic Prayer IV

Here we have a prayer with a set preface. This is quite unusual in the Roman tradition. The prayer is best used when no special preface is set for a particular occasion or on the Sundays in Ordinary Time. The prayer has no special formula for the dead.

Eucharistic Prayers for Reconciliation I and II

These two prayers were created for the 1975 Holy Year celebration. They were prepared in order to highlight our thanksgiving for various aspects of reconciliation. Since then, they have been available for use when the mystery of reconciliation has been a special theme of a Eucharistic celebration.

Eucharistic Prayers for Children I, II, and III

These three prayers are full Eucharistic Prayers but are couched in simpler language adapted to the needs of children. Their use is limited to Masses celebrated with children. One noteworthy feature of them is the relatively large number of acclamations they contain. These are provided to encourage active participation. Ultimately these texts are designed to enable young members of the faithful to participate more effectively in Masses celebrated with adults.

Eucharistic Prayer for Masses
for Various Needs and Occasions

This prayer—in four versions—is the most recent addition to our collection of Eucharistic Prayers. It came to us from the Swiss bishops, and was designed to fit various circumstances, complementing the Masses and Prayers for Various Needs and Occasions already in the *Roman Missal*. The prayer is designed to be prayed in one of four different ways, so it offers four different prefaces with corresponding intercessions. Some recommendations for their use are as follows:

a. "The Church on the Way to Unity": with formularies of Masses "For the Pope," "For a Council or Synod," and "For Pastoral or Spiritual Meetings," among others.

b. "God Guides the Church on the Way of Salvation": with formularies of Masses "For the Universal Church," "For the Laity," and "For the Family," among others.

c. "Jesus, Way to the Father": with formularies of Masses "For the Spread of the Gospel," "For

Persecuted Christians," and "For the Nation," among others.

d. "Jesus, the Compassion of God": with formularies of Masses "For Refugees and Exiles," "For Prisoners," and "For the Sick," among others.

Chapter 5

The Rite of Communion

THE ENTIRE LITURGY OF THE MASS comes to completion in Communion. This is the great gift that Jesus has left us. We have been brought into his presence through our assembling, the proclamation of the word, and the consecration of the bread and wine. We now take up his supper invitation and eat and drink from the table of the Lord. Why else would Jesus call us to bring to the altar and bless bread and wine if not for us to eat and drink them? They have no other purpose! This is why Communion at Mass should be from the bread and wine consecrated at that particular Mass (GIRM, no. 85).

This food is the very stuff of Christian living in the love of the Trinity. The words of John's Gospel should never be far from our thoughts:

> "Very truly, I tell you, unless you eat the flesh of the Son of Man and drink his blood, you have no life in you. Those who eat my flesh and drink my blood have eternal life, and I will raise them up on the last day; for my flesh is true food and my blood is true

> drink. Those who eat my flesh and drink my blood
> abide in me, and I in them" (6:53–56).

Here we have one of the most ancient elements of
Christian Eucharistic thought. Jesus teaches that
through our Communion we are one in him. This
unity in him brings us into unity with the Father and
the Spirit. It is also the promise of the fulfillment of all
things in Christ. We will be raised up. In fact, the
whole of creation will be made anew (Rom 8:19–23).
Our Communion in the Body and Blood of Christ is
an initial part of this final consummation of all things.

As we now begin our analysis of each of the parts
of the rite of Communion, an interesting point comes
to the fore. Almost every prayer in the rite has a direct
scriptural origin. It is almost as though human words
falter at this point, and the word of God guides us to
Communion in the Godhead.

The Our Father

The first historical evidence we have of the Lord's
Prayer in the Mass comes from the time of St.
Ambrose, Bishop of Milan (d. 397). The Gospels give
us two versions of the prayer (Mt 6:9–13 and Lk
11:2–4). The liturgy uses Matthew's text. The request
for daily bread motivates the placing of the prayer
before Communion. However, there is a petition for
forgiveness as well. This serves as part of our preparation for the sacred food. St. Augustine (354–430)
takes up this point in one of his sermons: "As a result

of these words we approach the altar with clean faces; with clean faces we share in the Body and Blood of Christ."[1]

This first prayer in the Communion rite has yet another dimension: a justice dimension. If God looks to nourish us, should we not look to feed the hungry? If God offers us forgiveness, should we not be a forgiving people? If, at Communion, we pray that God's kingdom come, doesn't our Communion call us to build that kingdom? In the Gospel of Matthew, the Lord's Prayer and the Beatitudes belong together in the one great Sermon on the Mount (see Mt 5:1–7:29). This is not the first time in the liturgy that we have been challenged to be mindful of the poor.

In the course of the history of its use in the liturgy, the Our Father, however, has not always been recited in the same manner. In the Churches in the East, and in Gaul, it was said in unison by the entire community. But this was not the case in Rome. Pope Gregory the Great (d. 604) considered the Our Father to be a prayer reserved to the presider. The priest sang the prayer, and the community ratified it with an Amen. In Spain, the congregation said *Amen* after each of the petitions, the individual verses being sung by the celebrant.

We now say the prayer as one body, the assembly, united in petition. There is provision for the Our Father, along with the parts that surround it, however, to be sung (GIRM, no. 81).

The Embolism: "Deliver us, Lord, from every evil..."

It appears that the embolism—an addition—dates from Pope Gregory the Great. It builds upon the final petition in the Lord's Prayer that God will deliver us from every evil. The closing lines seem to take their cue from the Letter to Titus: "... while we wait for the blessed hope and the manifestation of the glory of our great God and Savior, Jesus Christ" (2:13). Again we are reminded that our Communion at Mass opens onto the coming of Christ in all his glory and the fulfillment of all things.

The Acclamation: "For the kingdom..."

This is a very ancient liturgical acclamation. In fact, it seemed to be such an obvious conclusion to the Lord's Prayer that it is written as a conclusion to the prayer in some of the oldest manuscripts of Matthew's Gospel. Apparently the Scripture copyist simply thought it belonged there, so much had it become a part of Christian prayer. The formula is another doxology, singing again the assembly's praise of God.

This response of praise raises an intriguing question. What are the things that manifest God's kingdom, power, and glory? We are reminded of our discussion regarding the Lord's Prayer and the coming of the kingdom. Another answer is found in the Opening Prayer for the Twenty-Sixth Sunday in Ordinary Time. There, God's power is described in terms of mercy and forgiveness. God's power is so great and above our conceptions that it even dares to forgive and be merciful. So our Communion is a gracious act of God. How can we hold back from taking up this offer to eat and drink at the table of the Lord?

The Greeting of Peace

We give each other the peace of Christ, a different and greater peace than the world can offer (cf. Jn 14:27). We have already seen that the sign of peace has been part of the Mass since our very first record of it from Justin Martyr. It has a scriptural warrant from Matthew's Gospel:

> "So when you are offering your gift at the altar, if you remember that your brother or sister has something against you, leave your gift there before the altar and go; first be reconciled to your brother or sister, and then come and offer your gift" (5:23–24).

The sign of peace is the third gesture of kissing in the liturgy. The altar and *Book of the Gospels* have been kissed, and now we greet each other likewise. This gesture of reverence, respect, and warmth reveals to us a threefold presence of Christ: in the altar and the things of the altar, in the word, and in the assembly. The "kiss" is at once a profound theological action and a warm human gesture. This human dimension is brought out further by the instruction that the kiss of peace should be in accordance with the custom and practices of the local culture (GIRM, no. 82).

The sign of peace, however, has not always been held at this juncture in the Mass. As the excerpt from Justin Martyr shows, in some Churches it preceded the presentation of the gifts. This is in line with our scriptural quote: "when you are offering your gift at the altar...." However, in ancient Rome the exchange was delayed in the liturgy until the Communion rite. Pope Innocent I (d. 417) saw it as a way of putting the final seal on the Eucharistic Prayer:

> It is after that of which I may not speak that peace should be proclaimed according to rule. For it is clear that the people thereby give their consent to everything...that has gone before, since the peace puts its seal on the conclusion [of the Eucharistic prayer].[2]

The Breaking of the Bread

In the early Church, the Eucharist was known as the "breaking of the bread": "The bread that we break, is it not a sharing in the Body of Christ? Because there is one bread, we who are many are one body, for we all partake of the one bread" (1 Cor 10:16–17). The significance of this part of the rite in our contemporary liturgy though is somewhat lost. There is little symbolic value in the snapping of wafer-like bread. Also, too often the Communion for the faithful is retrieved from reserved hosts in the tabernacle. The admonition that all should receive from bread consecrated at *that* Mass is not given much consideration (GIRM, no. 85). Nevertheless, this part of the rite is a reminder of our place at the table where we become most profoundly the body of Christ through our participation in Communion.

The Rite of Commingling

The Missal gives no explanation of this rite—in which a piece of the host is broken off and placed in the chalice—and does not call too much attention to it. It simply remains as a part of our worship from ancient times. The rite however does give us an opportunity to look at two interesting parallel practices from the Church in Rome, at the Mass of the pope. At Communion time, some of the bread consecrated at the papal Mass was sent to the other churches in the city where the Eucharist was being celebrated. Known as the *fermentum,* the particle from the pope's Mass was consumed with the consecrated elements from the Masses of the suburban churches. The rite of Communion in those churches served, then, as a sign of the unity of the Church of the city as the body of Christ through Communion in the Body of Christ. By the seventh century it seems that this practice had become restricted to the Easter Vigil. It eventually fell out of use altogether.

While the *fermentum* custom signified unity across the city, a second papal custom symbolized unity between past and present. We have evidence from early in the eighth century of the pope setting aside a piece of the consecrated bread from the Sunday Eucharist. At the Mass on the next Sunday, celebrated in a different church in the city, he would place this reserved bread among the bread consecrated at that Mass. Through this he was able to symbolize the unity of the Church and its celebration from past to present. The practice, interesting and slightly odd, did not survive. Nor is it clear how widespread it was.

The Lamb of God

The Lamb of God or *Agnus Dei* is a chant, led by choir or cantor, with people responding. Alternatively, it may simply be recited (GIRM, no. 83). Unfortunately, this is one of those parts of the liturgy that the congregation often leaves to the presider to lead. That is not his role. The aim of the song is to accompany the breaking of the bread. The musical form of it allows for the verses to be repeated as many times as is necessary. It should continue for the duration of the breaking of the bread. The song is originally from Greek-speaking Syria. It was introduced into the Masses in Rome by Pope Sergius (687–701) who was a Syrian, though born in Palermo, Italy.

The text is deeply scriptural. The strongest reference is to the Book of Revelation: "Blessed are those who are invited to the marriage supper of the Lamb" (19:9). This takes up the image of Jesus as the Lamb, an image that John the Baptist applied to him: "Here is the Lamb of God who takes away the sin of the world!" (Jn 1:29). As we sing the chant we find ourselves in a sea of powerful images pointing toward being saved by God's actions. It was the blood of the lamb that saved the Israelites from the angel of death (Ex 12:13). The passing over of the avenging angel led to their freedom from slavery and their entry into the Promised Land of milk and honey. The sacrifice of the lamb also figures prominently in the fourth Servant Song of the Book of the Prophet Isaiah (Is 53:7–11). Paul describes Christ as our Passover Lamb (1 Cor 5:7). The First Letter of Peter does much the same: "You know that you were ransomed...with the precious blood of Christ, like that of a lamb without defect or blemish" (1:18–19). As we prepare to approach the table, we fill the air with the sounds of the mighty acts of God.

The Communion Procession

To receive the Body and Blood of Christ the faithful come in procession singing. The song starts when the presider takes Communion and continues until all have partaken. We sing out of joy and to express our unity (GIRM, no. 86). Following Communion the assembly enters a time of silence, prayer, and reflection on the great mystery of Christ, communion in him and communion with each other as his body. It is permissible at this time for the entire assembly to sing a psalm, canticle of praise, or hymn (GIRM, no. 88).

Contemporary Catholics are strongly aware of the doctrine of the Real Presence of Christ in the consecrated bread and wine. Yet the Communion procession reminds us of a complementary teaching that is worth retrieving. The early Christians were acutely aware that their Communion in Christ at the liturgy entailed their communion with one another as well. Communion had implications for community living and behavior. I will let the words of two of the great bishops and theologians of their day speak. The first is Augustine, Bishop of Hippo (354–430):

> If you are the body and members of Christ, then what is laid on the Lord's table is the sacrament of what you yourselves are, and it is the sacrament of what you are that you receive. It is to what you yourselves are that you answer "Amen," and this answer is your affidavit. Be a member of Christ's body, so that your "Amen" may be authentic.[3]

Theodore of Mopsuestia (c. 350–428) is even clearer. Significantly, he reminds us that our partipation in the Body and Blood of Christ leads us into the very life of the Trinity itself:

> By communion in the blessed mysteries we shall be united among ourselves and joined to Christ our Lord, whose body we believe ourselves to be, and through whom we become partakers of the divine nature.[4]

How to Receive Communion

The current liturgy allows for Communion in the Body of Christ either in the hand or on the tongue. Communion in the Blood of Christ is normally from the chalice. In all this it is worth remembering what the patristic writers said. They witness to the spiritual strengths of the earliest custom of receiving the Body of Christ in the hand, and of drinking from the cup, all the while standing. Our guide will be Cyril of Jerusalem (c. 315–386). He also mentions the interesting devotional action of touching the eyes with the consecrated bread. The following excerpt is from his teachings:

> When you approach, do not extend your hands with palms upward and fingers apart, but make your left hand a throne for your right hand, since the latter is to receive the King; then, while answering "Amen," receive the Body of Christ in the hollow of your hand. Next, carefully sanctify your eyes through contact with the sacred Body; then take it in your mouth, being watchful that nothing of it is lost. If you were to lose part of it, it would be like losing one of your own members. If someone were to give you some flakes of gold, would you not guard them very carefully and see to it that you did not lose any or suffer a loss? Should you not therefore watch far more carefully over an object more valuable than gold or precious stones, lest you lose a crumb of it? Then, after receiving the Body of Christ, approach his Blood....[5]

Communion to the Sick

The sick are also present to the assembly. They are in our thoughts and prayers. Their usual seats are left vacant. Yet we feel their absence. Our union with them is made concrete though when Communion is brought to them from the assembly. The Bread of Life is for the nourishment of all the members of the body of Christ.

Postcommunion Prayer

The Communion rite is brought to a close with the postcommunion prayer. Often this is misunderstood as the closing prayer of the Mass. This prayer, led by the presider, has two functions (GIRM, nos. 56h, 89). It brings to completion the petitions and prayers made by the assembly during the silence after the Communion processional song. And in doing so, it concludes the entire rite of Communion. Normally the prayer is quite short and to the point. Through it the community asks that God grant them the fruits of the great mystery they have just celebrated. Some prayers apply this to the present world, while others focus on the future when all things are taken up in Christ.

Unlike the Opening Prayer of Mass, there is no need for a period of silent petition after the presider has made the invitation "Let us pray." This is simply because the whole gathering have been taken up in silent petition and prayer following their reception of Communion.

Chapter 6

The Rites of Dismissal

THE DISMISSAL RITES WHICH CONCLUDE the Mass are simple and brief (GIRM, no. 90). Any announcements are read out, the stipulation being: only if they are necessary. The presider gives the blessing. There are various options available for the blessing if there is a special feast. The *Missal* also provides a selection of prayers over the people if the Sunday celebration requires further solemnity. The deacon or, in his absence, the presider sounds the dismissal.

The brevity of the dismissal rites should not be confused with their having nothing to say. The dismissal sends the members of the assembly—priest, deacon, baptized—out into the world to be what they have become in the Eucharist. Now we are called to transform the world as we have been transformed into Christ. We take with us the effects of the way grace has worked upon us in the liturgy. The word of God has been read and preached to us. We have prayed using the words of the foreign woman with the sick daughter. Our petitions for the world and the forgotten have been offered. We have proclaimed our thanksgiving in face of the real situation of our lives. Our hope in the coming of God's kingdom has been renewed. Finally we have been nourished by the Sacrament and become one in the Body of Christ. The Eucharistic liturgy ends with our taking up our place in the world as a Eucharistic people.

What about the final song? Strictly speaking, this is not a part of the Mass! The Mass ends when the assembly has responded to the deacon's sending forth: "Go in peace to love and serve the Lord." Instrumental music or a song may accompany any procession of the ministers as they leave the church. However, the liturgy has come to a close, and it is time to give witness to our thanksgiving.

Chapter 7
Posture and Gesture

IN THE EUCHARIST WE PRAY with our bodies. There are a number of gestures and postures that are part and parcel of our liturgical prayer. It is refreshing to take an occasional look at their significance. Here we shall examine four of the most important ones: standing, kissing, kneeling, and processing.

Standing

The first and most important liturgical posture is standing. For centuries, before pews and kneelers were ever considered to be desirable or necessary, the early Christians willingly stood to pray. This may seem overly bold—standing in petition before the living God. However, our ancestors in faith were conscious of the dignity that God had given them as adopted children. Because of God's generous grace and mercy, they stood before God, arms outstretched, to pray. This was especially so in the liturgy. Origen (d. 254) describes the situation as follows:

Even more than stretching out the hands to heaven, one must lift up the soul heavenward. More than raising up the eyes, one must lift up the spirit to God. For there can be no doubt that among a thousand possible positions of the body, outstretched hands and uplifted eyes are to be preferred above all others, so imaging forth in the body those directions of the soul which are fitting in prayer. We are of the opinion that this posture should be preferred, where there is nothing to prevent it, for there are certain circumstances, such as sickness, where we may pray even sitting or lying.[1]

This tradition is reflected in the *General Instruction of the Roman Missal,* which sets out that the faithful should stand to pray the Eucharistic Prayer, with an option to kneel or bow during the consecration. The *Instruction* however also admits an acceptance of the practice of kneeling from the Holy, Holy, Holy onward (GIRM, no. 43). We have already seen other interpretations of the posture of standing. When we stand for the Gospel, we stand as servants before the Lord, and we stand in readiness to do the word of God.

Kissing

The gesture of kissing in the liturgy is a mark of reverence and respect. Three things are kissed in the Mass, each one corresponding to one of the modes by which Christ is present in the liturgy. The presider, deacon, and ordained kiss the *altar* at the beginning and at the end of Mass. The altar has often been seen as a symbol of Christ. The *Book of the Gospels* is kissed by the deacon, an act of reverence toward Christ present in the word. And the *members of the faithful* exchange a kiss of peace in a gesture performed according to local custom. With Christ present in their midst, those who have gathered in his name offer to one another his peace.

Kneeling

Kneeling, a posture closely related to kissing, was very rare in the early liturgy. It did not make its appearance in the Mass until the thirteenth century. Its insertion was in response to an understanding of the Mass that was too focused on sin rather than on whole-hearted thanksgiving for God's gracious actions in Christ. Kneeling however had been common earlier in private prayer. Two senses can be attached to it. Along with prostration and genuflection, kneeling could embody intense petition and supplication. This is why kneeling was incorporated into the Good Friday petitions. Kneeling also took hold as the appropriate gesture for reverence. Gradually throughout medieval times it became the favored posture for the laity during the Eucharistic Prayer in the churches of Western Europe. This brought about a slightly strange anomaly. The traditional Eucharistic Prayer described the people as standing around the altar, while in fact they had stopped standing and were kneeling instead.

Processing

The Roman liturgy has always been keen on processions. We find this hard to imagine because our current churches are too encumbered with pews and furnishings. Yet the Mass has a number of processions: the entry of the presider and ministers, the carrying of the *Book of the Gospels,* the presentation of the gifts, and the Communion procession. Processions bring a sense of movement and color to the liturgy. Their musical accompaniment adds the dimensions of sound and unity that comes with singing. While the entrance procession brings completion and wholeness to the assembly, the procession to the table for Communion offers a tangible expression of our oneness with each other in Christ.

Chapter 8

Music in the Liturgy

A LOT OF TIME AND ENERGY IS TAKEN UP in discussions on what is going to be sung in a liturgy and when. Two questions, however, can bring much needed clarity to the exchange. One is: What parts of the rite entail singing? The second is about the quality of music chosen: What factors determine whether a particular piece of music is suitable?

A number of parts that make up the rite of the Mass are actually acclamations. They are prayed best, and most authentically, when sung. These acclamations are musical forms and express our praise of God. The Gospel acclamation is clearly one of them. There are also a number in the Eucharistic Prayer: the *Sanctus* (Holy, Holy, Holy), the memorial acclamation ("Let us proclaim the mystery of faith"), the doxology ("through him, with him, in him..."), and the Amen.

The psalm is one of the musical elements in the Liturgy of the Word. It is sung by the cantor or psalmist from the ambo. There are numerous musical settings for each of the psalms. A common psalm may also be sung throughout a particular liturgical season.

Other musical forms are litanies, such as the *Kyrie eleison* ("Lord, have mercy") and the Lamb of God. Extra invocations can be added to these when necessary to ensure they accompany the ritual actions for their full duration.

The processions seem more fitting and alive too when accompanied by music. The entrance procession and the Communion procession are heightened with songs that are suitable to that particular action. The songs can be seasonal or related to the particular feast. However, they should end when the procession comes to a close. However, some songs suitable for these processions are written in such a way that they only make sense when the whole piece is sung right through. When used at the beginning of Mass it would be best to delay the entrance of the procession until well into the song. For the procession of gifts, a song or instrumental piece may accompany the action.

Finally, a liturgy planning group could give attention to those parts of the rite which may be sung, even though their literary genre or place in the liturgy does not actually require a musical setting. Included here are: the set of prayers comprising the invitation to the Lord's Prayer, the prayer itself, the embolism, and the concluding doxology; a hymn, psalm, or song of praise after Communion; and a closing hymn.

Occasionally the solemn nature of a particular celebration is enhanced with sung greetings, readings, and Eucharistic Prayer.

Clearly the rite of the Mass invites us to participate strongly with song and music, but also to do so appropriately. How do we make such our choices? A document released by the United States Bishops' Committee on Liturgy called *Music in Catholic Worship* (first ed., 1972; 2nd, 1983) provides some much needed help. It suggests music be chosen according to three judgments: musical, liturgical, and pastoral. The bishops recognize that the function of music in the liturgy is to enhance the full, active, and conscious participation of all worshipers in the Mass. Accordingly, music must serve—never dominate or distract. The musical judgment asks whether a piece is technically, aesthetically, and expressively good. However, the pursuit of excellence should not be overplayed. The document quotes Augustine: "Do not allow yourselves to be offended by the imperfect while you strive for the perfect." The second judgment is the liturgical one. The nature of the liturgical forms and genres themselves helps determine what kind of music is called for, what parts are to be preferred for singing, and who is to sing them. Thirdly comes the pastoral judgment. It governs the use and function of *every* element in the celebration. It asks whether the music chosen will enable the people in the assembly to express their faith in this place, in this age, in this culture. Ideally, the pastoral judgment is made by the preparation team.

Music in the liturgy means more than providing a couple of hymns and reflection pieces. It is integral to the celebration. The singing is the responsibility of the entire assembly. Various ministers are required, ranging from musicians, cantors, and choir members to conductors, all there to support the singing of the assembly. The community needs preparation, resources, and training. Far too often we have added music to the liturgy based on our own preferences. It is now time to allow the music in the rite itself to be expressed, and to allow the pastoral situation of the assembly and the liturgy to come together in this act of praise.

Chapter 9

Major Periods in the Development of Our Liturgy: A Thumbnail Sketch

THROUGHOUT THIS BOOK we have traveled across whole centuries, covered empires, and dipped into particular cities and regions. The history of Mass as celebrated by Roman Catholics down the centuries demands such a panorama. The Eucharist as a liturgy has always been responsive to the people and cultures who prayed it. The Church of Rome has also happily borrowed from other Christian Churches, a witness to the "catholic" nature of our worship. Below is a rather simple thumbnail sketch of the major periods of this development. It is not meant as an exhaustive treatise, but simply as a guide across two millennia.

Within the Memory of the Apostles: 34–312

While we do not have a vast amount of information about this period, nevertheless it is the most important for the establishment of the structure of the Mass. By and large the focus of the liturgy was the house church. Yet, as Christian groups grew, and the persecutions became more sporadic, larger groups formed. This gave rise to a need for public buildings for worship. From the house churches sprang the three most central parts of Christian communal prayer: the liturgies of Baptism and Eucharist and the Book of the Scriptures. Also, the Christian week took shape. It had a focus on Sunday Eucharist, fasting on Wednesday and Friday, and morning and evening prayer each weekday. The seasons of Lent and Easter became established, along with the celebration of the feast days of martyrs. This period also covers the origins of Church leadership as we know it today, with the development of the office of overseer (*episcopus* or bishop) along with a group of elders *(presbyters)*.

The Religion of the Empire: 313–600

The persecutions came to an end with the conversion of Emperor Constantine and, specifically, with his Edict of Milan in 313. Later, in 380, Emperor Theodosius made Christianity the official religion of the empire. Freedom from violence and support from the state coffers brought many changes to Christian worship. With government funds came public worship and a new form of worship space, the basilica. Consequently, when the Eucharist of the house church was celebrated in newly constructed, grand buildings, it became a more elaborate affair. By the fifth century, the key liturgical furnishings in the churches—the ambo, the presider's chair, and the altar table—became permanent features. A great array of liturgical books were created too—books for the presider, the master of ceremonies, the epistle reader, the Gospel reader, the cantor, and the choir. This variety is testimony to the many ministries in the liturgy and their integrity. But we are more used to experiencing all these roles being exercised by one or two ministers only.

In Rome an important change took place. As a response to the change in culture, there was a change in liturgical language. Up until the mid fourth century the Romans worshiped in Greek. From then on, they moved across to the newly dominant Latin. With the change in language came the creation of whole new types of prayer which became possible with the different structure, style, and vocabulary of Latin. It is difficult for us to comprehend that the original language of the Church of Rome was Greek! The general rule throughout the Christian world was that Christians worshiped in their own language, or the language of the culture in which they lived. They also worshiped in the style and traditions of their own local church, giving rise to a rich profusion of prayers and rites, which all displayed a unity of purpose. Unity in belief was most important. Diversity of practice was seen as a witness to this one faith.

Along with the language differences came an increase in devotional activity. Processions, fasts, vigils, feasts, and the cult of the martyrs all flourished during this period. One of the less felicitous trends of this period was the decline in the number of the faithful who received Communion.

From the Tribes to the Sixteenth Century: 600–1500

The slow continual decline in the fortunes of the city of Rome and the rupturing of the Roman Empire in the West did not bring about the end of the Church nor its liturgy. As the various Germanic tribes gained ascendancy across what today we call Europe, they oversaw new approaches to worship. By the dawn of the sixteenth century, Catholic worship at Mass had become radically different from that of the year 600. What took place over this period? For the first time in the history of Christian liturgy, the Mass was not adapted to respond to the change in the language of the people. As the various European languages emerged, the Mass stayed in Latin. The theology of priesthood however underwent modification. With the gradual enforcement of the new policy of clerical celibacy, the tradition of married clergy disappeared. The priest was seen to be more of a sacral figure, with control over the sacred, and increasingly arcane, liturgy.

The liturgy itself continued to develop, though it was little understood by priests and people alike because it was in Latin. Each major diocese or region or monastery had its own form of the Mass, often a combination of local and imported forms. But not all were successful. Yet diversity remained the norm.

While lay people were sidelined from understanding the prayers, making responses, understanding the readings, and receiving Communion, something new emerged. Their devotional life intensified to make up for their exclusion. They came to understand the Mass as an allegory of Christ's life. From the thirteenth century onward, they wholeheartedly took up Eucharistic devotions. If they could not eat the Bread of Life, they certainly wanted their eyes to be sated with it! Emerging from this time were the feast of *Corpus Christi,* Eucharistic processions, benediction, and the development of prayer before the reserved Blessed Sacrament.

The Council of Trent (1545–63) to the Second Vatican Council (1962–65)

The reforms of the Council of Trent continue to mark our worship today. The Reformation was a time of bitter polemic, both Protestant and Catholic. The Protestant leaders attacked in particular the theology and practice of the Mass and the priesthood. The Catholic response was to focus on those issues that were under siege. The result was that, after much debate, the bishops in the Council reaffirmed Latin as the language of the liturgy. They sought to curb some of the abuses they found, and sought more uniformity of liturgical practice. However, a good number of different traditions for celebrating the Mass remained, notably in the dioceses of Milan, Paris, and Lyons to name just a few, and among religious orders such as the Dominicans. The Mass was reinforced as a clerical affair, with the laity participating by attendance only. The Council of Trent and, later, the Roman Curia, continually sought the people to return to the reception of frequent Communion, but it took some three hundred years for bishops to promote this reform. As with the medieval period, the faith of the laity continued to be nourished by devotions, though now they were more carefully scrutinised.

Theologically and liturgically, this era was held captive to the narrow and polemical debates between the Catholic and Protestant churches. Yet toward the close of the nineteenth century, there emerged a group of scholars committed to retrieving some of the richness of the theology and liturgy of the early Church. Eventually, this budding "liturgical movement," as it came to be known, offered a vision of liturgy that was theologically broader and more attentive pastorally than the Reformation polemic.

Vatican II and Beyond

The Second Vatican Council both continued the development of the Mass initiated by the Council of Trent and reformed the Mass in light of the contemporary world and the insights from the great liturgies and theologians of the tradition. The first document of the Council was the *Constitution on the Sacred Liturgy*. It set the foundations for the reform of the

Eucharist, resulting in the following prominent features of our current liturgy: celebration in the language of the people; the upholding of the integrity of the different ministers and ministries; and interaction among the members of the assembly, rather than the segregation of clergy from the laity.

In summary, *all* the faithful are now called to full, conscious, and active participation in worship. It has been the hope of this little work that its readers, and author too, will be stimulated and encouraged to pursue this profound teaching.

Notes

Acknowledgments

1. Adolf Adam. *The Eucharistic Celebration: The Source and Summit of Faith* (Collegeville, MN: The Liturgical Press, 1994), 6–7. Translation by Robert C. Schultz.

Chapter 2
The Liturgy of the Word

1. *In Isaiam, Prologus (Corpus Christianorum)*, Ser. Lat. Vol. 63, p.1, quoted in Lucien Deiss, *The Mass* (Collegeville: Liturgical Press, 1992), 34.

2. Joseph Jungmann, *The Mass of the Roman Rite,* Vol. I (Westminster, Md: Christian Classics Inc., 1992), 448–9.

3. Thomas Merton, *The Wisdom of the Desert* (London: Hollis and Carter, 1961), xxxiv.

4. "Some Questions Regarding Collaboration of Non-ordained Faithful in Priests" Sacred Ministry, Article 3, "The Homily," no. 2, in *Origins 27*, no. 24 (November 27, 1997).

Chapter 4
The Eucharistic Prayer

1. The Latin text for the assembly's response is *Dignum et iustum est.*

Chapter 5
The Rite of Communion

1. Augustine *Sermon 17, 5, 5.* See A. G. Martimort, *The Church at Prayer. Vol II. The Eucharist,* new ed., edited by R. Cabié (Collegeville: Liturgical Press, 1986), 109.

2. *Epistle 25 ad Decentium,* quoted in Cabié, *The Church at Prayer. Vol II. The Eucharist,* 114.

3. Augustine, *Sermon 272* (PL 38:1247), quoted by Cabié, *The Church at Prayer. Vol II. The Eucharist,* 118.

4. Theodore of Mopsuestia, *Baptismal Homily 5:13.* English translation in Edward Yarnold, *The Awe-Inspiring Rites of Initiation: Baptismal Homilies of the Fourth Century* (Slough: St. Pauls, 1972), 247.

5. Cyril of Jerusalem (c. 315–386), *Catecheses mystagogicae* V 27 (*SC* 126:170–3) quoted by Cabié, *The Church at Prayer. Vol II. The Eucharist,* 120.

Chapter 7
Posture and Gesture

1. Origen, *De Oratione, 31, 2.* Quoted in John K. Leonard and Nathan D. Mitchell, *The Postures of the Assembly During the Eucharistic Prayer* (Chicago: Liturgy Training Publications, 1994), 23.

Glossary

ambo: Also known as the *lectern*: the place of proclamation of the word of God and the focal point for the faithful during the Liturgy of the Word. From it, the readings are read, the psalm sung, the homily delivered, and the general intercessions offered. The Easter Exultet is also proclaimed from the ambo. It is one of the three furnishings in the sanctuary, taking its prominent place in concert with the altar and the presider's chair. It is normally fixed rather than moveable and positioned so the ministers of the word may be seen and heard easily. Because of the dignity of the ambo's function, it should not be used as a merely convenient place for making announcements or directives.

Ambrose (c. 339–397): Bishop of Milan, and a famous preacher and theologian. His writings contain many interesting descriptions of early liturgical practices. He was an important influence on St. Augustine.

Arianism: Heresy from the fourth century maintaining that Jesus was not divine, but simply the first born of all creatures. The Councils of Nicea (325) and Constantinople (381) concentrated on providing a theological response, known to us through the Nicene Creed. Despite the Councils, however, Arianism remained widespread during the fifth century among the peoples who conquered large parts of the Roman Empire.

asperges: The rite of blessing and sprinkling with holy water; an option in the Introductory Rites of the Mass. It carries the sense of cleansing and forgiveness that are based in the waters of Baptism. Its name comes from the Latin verb meaning "to sprinkle."

Augustine (354–430): Bishop of Hippo in North Africa. He is perhaps the most influential theologian in the entire history of the Church of the West. His collected works are vast and include many sermons that contain interesting liturgical information.

basilica: Early form of church building modeled on public meeting halls also called "basilica." Today, the title "basilica" is a privileged one, given to prominent churches.

Book of the Gospels: The ancient and medieval Church book specifically designed for the proclamation of the Gospel. The *Book of Kells* is a famous example, perhaps more renowned for the quality of its artwork rather than its liturgical use. Our reformed liturgy has a place for a *Book of the Gospels*. If it is brought in as part of the entrance procession, it is laid on the altar. During the *Alleluia* verse before the Gospel, the deacon (or priest) carries it in procession from the altar to the ambo.

collect: Term often used for the Opening Prayer of Mass. However it is also a general term for the genre of prayers which includes the Prayer over the Gifts, the Post-Communion Prayer, and the optional Prayer over the People, as well as the Opening Prayer.

Constitution on the Sacred Liturgy: The first document produced by the bishops of the Second Vatican Council (December 4, 1963). It deals with the reform of the liturgy of the Catholic Church.

Council of Trent: Council of the Church that met for many sessions between 1545 and 1563. It established the basis for the renewal of the Catholic Church as a response to the condition of the Church itself and the spread of Protestantism.

Creed: Also known as the *symbolum*, the symbol: while the final text of the Creed takes its name from the Councils of Nicea (325) and Constantinople (381), it originated as a baptismal creed.

Cyril of Jerusalem (c. 315–386): Bishop of Jerusalem. Preserved from among his works are a series of Lenten and Easter instructions for those who were undertaking Baptism.

Directory for Masses with Children (DMC): Document providing and describing the application of and fundamental principles for celebrating Mass with children. It has provisions for when children are a part of the assembly, as well as for when they make up the bulk of the assembly. Following broad consultation with bishops' conferences across the world, the document was produced in 1973 by the then *Congregation for Divine Worship* (now named the *Congregation for Divine Worship and the Discipline of the Sacraments*). The document is published in *The Liturgy Documents: A Parish Resource* (Chicago: Liturgy Training Publications).

Edict of Milan (313): Edict of Emperor Constantine marking the acceptance of Christianity as a legal religion in the Roman Empire.

Eucharist: From the Greek word for "thanksgiving," it is one of the oldest terms for the Mass. As well, the phrase "Liturgy of the Eucharist" is used to designate the part of the Mass that includes the Preparation of the Gifts, the Prayer of Thanksgiving, and Communion.

Exultet: The proclamation of the Easter faith sung by a deacon during the liturgy of the Easter Vigil.

General Intercessions: Also known as the *Prayer of the Faithful* and the *universal prayer:* through these prayers, made in response to the Liturgy of the Word, the faithful exercise their baptismal office by offering prayers to God for the salvation of all.

***General Introduction to the Lectionary for Mass* (GIL):** Official Church document setting out the principles and norms for the interpretation of the *Lectionary* for Mass. It is found at the front of the *Lectionary.* The document is published in *The Liturgy Documents: A Parish Resource* (Chicago: Liturgy Training Publications).

General Instruction of the Roman Missal (GIRM): Official Church document setting out the principles and norms for the interpretation of the Mass. It is found at the front of the Missal. The document is published in *The Liturgy Documents: A Parish Resource* (Chicago: Liturgy Training Publications).

Gregory the Great (c. 540–604): Pope, theologian, and writer. He made important changes to the liturgy of the city of Rome. His encouragement of liturgical music led to his name being given to a particular form of singing—*Gregorian chant.*

Innocent I (d. 417): He was elected pope in 402. His letter to Decentius of Gubbio offers insights into some of the liturgical practices in the city of Rome during the early fifth century.

Jerome (c. 342–420): A renowned biblical scholar. His translation of the Bible into Latin, subsequently known as the *Vulgate,* was the standard Latin version of the Scriptures in the West.

Justin Martyr (c. 100–c.165): One of the earliest Christian thinkers and writers. His works contain some of the first descriptions of the practices and beliefs around Baptism and the Eucharist.

Kyrie eleison: The Greek name for a prayer in the form of a litany that is part of the Introductory Rites of the Mass. Today, in English-language Masses, it is known as the Lord, Have Mercy. Although the Mass was already being said in Latin when this prayer was added to the liturgy, it was not translated into Latin but remained in Greek.

Lectionary: The liturgical book containing all the readings for each Mass. The *Sunday Lectionary* has three volumes, reflecting the three-year cycle of readings. The *Weekday Lectionary* has two volumes for its two-year cycle. The *General Introduction to the Lectionary* is found at the front of the first volume of each of the *Sunday* and *Weekday Lectionaries.*

litany: A repetitive form of intercessory prayer. Usually, the cantor sings the various petitions to which the assembly sings a set response.

liturgy: The public prayer of the Church.

Liturgy of the Hours: The daily public prayer of the Church made up of psalms, readings, hymns, intercessions, prayers, antiphons, and responses.

***Music in Catholic Worship* (MCW):** Official document of the United States Bishops' Committee on Liturgy that suggests principles to guide the choice of music to be used in the liturgy. The document is published in *The Liturgy Documents: A Parish Resource* (Chicago: Liturgy Training Publications).

Missal: See *Roman Missal.*

Ordinary Time: The time celebrating the mystery of our salvation in Christ in general. It underpins the seasons—Advent, Christmas, Lent, and Easter—which celebrate particular facets of this mystery.

Origen (c. 185–254): He was perhaps the first of the great Scripture scholars, theologians, and spiritual writers. Many of his numerous works have unfortunately been lost.

passion: The suffering of Jesus, especially his physical suffering, but also his mental and spiritual anguish and social marginalization.

presider's chair: One of the three permanent furnishings in the sanctuary of a church building. Alongside the ambo and altar, the chair is a symbol of the leadership of the assembly. It is the place from which the presider leads the Introductory Rites and the rites of dismissal, as well as the Post-Communion Prayer. The homily may be delivered from this place too. While the deacon sits next to the presider, other ministers and servers sit quite separately.

rite: A particular liturgical action or sequence of related actions, for example, the Introductory Rites.

Roman Canon: The alternative name for Eucharistic Prayer I.

Roman Missal: The official text of the Mass liturgy. It is made up of the *Lectionary* and the *Sacramentary*. However, the term is often used to mean the *Sacramentary* alone. Our study of the Mass is based on the Latin edition of the Missal released in 2002. This is the third edition since the renewal of the liturgy after Vatican II.

rubrics: The directions for a particular part of a rite. They are printed in red in ritual books.

Sacramentary: Book containing the prayers, rites, rubrics, and options for the celebration of Mass. At the front of the book is the *General Instruction of the Roman Missal,* along with pastoral notes from the local conference of bishops. The *Sacramentary* is complemented by the *Lectionary.*

Second Vatican Council: The second assembly of the Catholic bishops of the world at the Vatican, held over four sessions between 1962 and 1965.

Theodore of Mopsuestia (c. 350–428): Bishop of Mopsuestia. His scriptural and theological writings contain insights into the liturgical practices of his day.

Resources for Further Exploration

Church Documents

The following major liturgical documents are all readily available in any edition of the following collection: *The Liturgy Documents: A Parish Resource.* Chicago: Liturgy Training Publications.

General Instruction of the Roman Missal (GIRM)

General Introduction to the Lectionary (GIL)

Directory for Masses with Children (DMC)

Music in Catholic Worship (MCW)

Other Books and Resources

Celebrating the Eucharist in Schools. A school-based professional development program produced by the Parramatta Diocesan Liturgy Commission and Catholic Education Office, Parramatta, 2000.

Chupungco, Anscar, ed. *Handbook for Liturgical Studies. Vol III. The Eucharist.* Collegeville: Liturgical Press, 1999.

Congregation for Divine Worship and the Discipline of the Sacraments. *Redemptionis Sacramentum (Instruction on Certain Matters to Be Observed or to Be Avoided Regarding the Most Holy Eucharist)*. Boston: Pauline Books & Media, 2003.

Deiss, Lucien. *The Mass*. Collegeville: Liturgical Press, 1992.

Deiss, Lucien. *The Word*. Collegeville: Liturgical Press, 1993.

———— *Visions of Liturgy and Music for a New Century*. Collegeville: Liturgical Press, 1996.

Donghi, Antonio. *Actions and Words: Symbolic Language and the Liturgy*. Collegeville: Liturgical Press, 1997.

Emminghaus, Johannes H. *The Eucharist: Essence, Form, Celebration*. Collegeville: Liturgical Press, 1997.

Huck, Gabe and Gerald T. Chinchar. *Liturgy with Style and Grace*. Chicago: Liturgy Training Publications, 1998.

Irwin, Kevin W. *Responses to 101 Questions on the Mass*. New York: Paulist Press, 1999.

John Paul II. *Dies Domini* (*On Keeping the Lord's Day Holy*). Boston: Pauline Books & Media, 2000.

———— *Ecclesia de Eucharistia* (*On the Eucharist in Its Relationship to the Church*). Boston: Pauline Books & Media, 2003.

Jungmann, Joseph A. *The Mass of the Roman Rite*. Vols 1 and II. Westminster, Md: Christian Classics, 1992.

Leonard, John K. and Nathan D. Mitchell. *The Postures of the Assembly During the Eucharistic Prayer.* Chicago: Liturgy Training Publications, 1994.

Martimort, A. G. *The Church at Prayer. Vol II. The Eucharist.* Edited by R. Cabié. New edition. Collegeville: Liturgical Press, 1986.

Miller, Charles E. *Liturgy for the People of God. Vol II. The Celebration of the Eucharist.* New York: Alba House, 2001.

Moore, Gerard. *A Study of the Mass.* Four audio tapes. North Strathfield, NSW: Build on the Rock, 1997.

———— *Eucharist and Justice.* Catholic Social Justice Series, no. 39. North Sydney: Australian Catholic Social Justice Council, 2000.

Press, Margaret, ed. *The Eucharist: Faith and Worship.* Strathfield: St. Pauls, 2001.

Smolarski, Dennis. *Q & A: The Mass.* Chicago: Liturgy Training Publications, 2002.

BOOKS & MEDIA

The Daughters of St. Paul operate book and media centers at the following addresses. Visit, call or write the one nearest you today, or find us on the World Wide Web, www.pauline.org

CALIFORNIA
3908 Sepulveda Blvd, Culver City, CA 90230 — 310-397-8676
5945 Balboa Avenue, San Diego, CA 92111 — 858-565-9181

FLORIDA
145 S.W. 107th Avenue, Miami, FL 33174 — 305-559-6715

HAWAII
1143 Bishop Street, Honolulu, HI 96813 — 808-521-2731
Neighbor Islands call: — 866-521-2731

ILLINOIS
172 North Michigan Avenue, Chicago, IL 60601 — 312-346-4228

LOUISIANA
4403 Veterans Memorial Blvd, Metairie, LA 70006 — 504-887-7631

MASSACHUSETTS
885 Providence Hwy, Dedham, MA 02026 — 781-326-5385

MISSOURI
9804 Watson Road, St. Louis, MO 63126 — 314-965-3512

NEW JERSEY
561 U.S. Route 1, Wick Plaza, Edison, NJ 08817 — 732-572-1200

NEW YORK
150 East 52nd Street, New York, NY 10022 — 212-754-1110

PENNSYLVANIA
9171-A Roosevelt Blvd, Philadelphia, PA 19114 — 215-676-9494

SOUTH CAROLINA
243 King Street, Charleston, SC 29401 — 843-577-0175

TENNESSEE
4811 Poplar Avenue, Memphis, TN 38117 — 901-761-2987

TEXAS
114 Main Plaza, San Antonio, TX 78205 — 210-224-8101

VIRGINIA
1025 King Street, Alexandria, VA 22314 — 703-549-3806

CANADA
3022 Dufferin Street, Toronto, ON M6B 3T5 — 416-781-9131

¡También somos su fuente para libros,
videos y música en español!